Sugar-Free Desserts,

Elbie Lebrecht has written two previous books and taught a number of courses on cooking without sugar and additives. She has degrees in politics and librarianship and runs a private picture library. She lives in London with her husband and three daughters.

by the same author

SUGAR-FREE CAKES AND BISCUITS
LIVING WITHOUT SUGAR

Sugar-Free Desserts, Drinks and Ices

*Recipes for Diabetics
and Dieters*

ELBIE LEBRECHT

faber and faber
LONDON · BOSTON

First published in 1993 by
Faber and Faber Limited
3 Queen Square London WC1N 3AU

Photoset by Wilmaset Ltd, Wirral
Printed by Cox & Wyman Ltd, Reading, Berkshire

A CIP record for this book is available from the
British Library

ISBN 0–571–16645–8

2 4 6 8 10 9 7 5 3 1

Contents

Acknowledgements

Jasmine Challis, senior dietitian at University College, London, gave me invaluable help in checking the carbohydrate and calorie counts and compiling the food table.

Professor W.P.T. James of the Rowett Research Unit in Aberdeen and Chairman of the WHO report on *Diet, Nutrition and Prevention of Chronic Disease* (1990), Dr W. K. Heaton of the Department of Medicine of the University of Bristol, Dr J. M. Graham of the Department of Health, Dr R. Lefever and Annie Cushing of Action and Information on Sugars helped clarify points that arose in the Introduction. Dr Erik Millstone of the Science Policy Research Unit of Sussex University provided useful advice with the section on Artificial Sweeteners.

Many appreciative thanks to all the tasters, both family and friends, who sampled recipes at the creation stage. My three daughters and husband undertook a large amount of the testing and their pithy remarks were always constructive.

Introduction

In 1985, when I wrote *Sugar-Free Cakes and Biscuits*, the assertion that sugar was intrinsically harmful to health was treated as freakish or cultish. It might not be good for diabetics, people said, but it cannot hurt anyone else.

Eight years is a long time in health awareness. Today, sugar has become an acknowledged public health enemy, attacked by a succession of government reports and joining tobacco as a threat to life. The information fight against tobacco has effectively been won: virtually every adult now knows that smoking causes lung cancer and a spate of other diseases. The focus is turning on sugar, which is increasingly seen as one of the greatest killers of all. Sugar and fat are the prime dietary sources of obesity, which causes heart disease, arteriosclerosis, diabetes and various cancers. The message emanating ever more powerfully from official sources is: if you want to live, cut down sugar to at least half of the present average consumption. Better still, cut it out altogether.

The food manufacturing industry does not like this one little bit, because most processed foods rely on sugar to give taste and texture, and governments are loath to offend such mighty revenue producers. But the statistics from local health authorities are incontrovertible. Too many people are dying prematurely because their diet is unhealthy. Obesity kills, and sugar is one of the two culprits implicated in the scandal. It also causes painful and disfiguring dental caries.

Health propaganda was directed initially at saturated fats, and awareness of the dangers of high cholesterol levels has risen. Twenty years ago, butter outsold margarine by a factor of three to one. Today people buy three times as much margarine as butter. Oil has replaced lard in many homes.

The message on sugar has lagged slightly behind fat. There is a widespread perception that something as 'nice' as a chocolate biscuit can surely not be bad. There is also a justifiable anxiety that eliminating sugar will leave unslaked cravings for sweeteners.

Yet sugar is, if anything, more culpable than fat. Unlike fat, it provides no nutritional benefit whatever: no vitamins, no minerals, no protein, no fibre. All those good things disappear in the 90 per cent of the plant that is discarded in the industrial process of refining sugar. 'Table sugar is one of the purest chemicals produced in large quantities by modern industry,' wrote R. Passmore and M. A. Eastwood in *Human Nutrition and Dietetics*. All it gives are calories, and excessive calories make you fat. It does not fill you up, or give more than a flash of energy, soon depleted. Nutritionally, it is worthless.

'But sugar gives you energy – everyone needs it!' solemnly declare the sugar bureaux of the world. We all do need energy, but the healthy way to get it is from complex or unrefined carbohydrates such as wholewheat flour, wholegrains, pulses, vegetables and fruit with its skin. When you eat refined sugar, white or brown, you get a raw burst of energy, then a drop into tiredness. Because the sugar is so processed it is not digested slowly by the body but rushes into the bloodstream, raising the blood sugar level. More insulin is produced in the pancreas (of non-diabetics) to take the sugar out of the blood, but the subsequent drop in blood sugar makes you feel tired and low; you need more sugar to pick you up.

Compare this with the feeling you get after eating an unrefined carbohydrate like a banana, something Wimbledon tennis champions knock back between fierce bouts of volleys and serves. The food is digested and released into the bloodstream slowly because of the fibre content. The result is a sustained energy, avoiding the roller-coaster effect of sugar.

Even worse, sugar is probably addictive. 'People who have multiple addictions find that giving up sugar and white flour is just as difficult as giving up cocaine,' writes Dr Robert Lefever, a specialist in treating eating disorders.

Unfortunately, in the case of sugar, there is no obvious alternative. Brown sugar differs very little from white sugar – it, too, has had 90 per cent of the original plant removed. It is nutritionally identical to white sugar in that it is a concentrated carbohydrate which contains no fibre at all. Health-cookery writers who use wholewheat flour and whole grains in their recipes but advocate raw cane or muscavado sugar are guilty of wishful and woolly thinking.

Wholewheat flour is milled from the whole grain but fibre is removed from all sugars at an early stage of refining. If you really wanted to eat unrefined sugar you would have to champ your way through several feet of sugar cane. Sugar juice is extracted from the crushed canes and is concentrated, crystallized and purified. Raw cane sugar contains some minerals because it has not been purified to the same degree as white sugar. However, the amount of mineral salts it contains is limited – about 0.5 per cent. You would have to eat a lot to get a reasonable amount of mineral intake. Raw cane sugar is the raw material shipped to Britain for purifying; the range of white sugar it contains is between 98.4 and 98.8 per cent. Muscavado sugar is usually made from 84–89 per cent white sugar, often sugar beet, which has been coated with a small percentage of molasses.

Honey is not as concentrated as sugar, containing 76.4 per cent sugars per 100 grams, but it contains no fibre and very few nutrients, and consequently is not used in my recipes. Although many people extol its virtues and mistakenly describe food made with it as sugar-free, it contains only minute amounts of two B vitamins and no others. It has very small amounts of minerals, including some trace minerals. Like sugar it was used in the Middle Ages as a medicine, and perhaps this is why it is still regarded as having special properties. People who spread it thickly over their bread as a substitute for jam are not improving their health. Honey has never been eaten as a basic food, but always used sparingly. Nature made it so difficult to obtain that we must assume it was never intended for large-scale consumption. It also has the same effect as sugar on the diabetic constitution.

Laboratories around the world have offered a variety of artificial sweeteners, some less unsafe than others. What they all have in common is that they are synthetic products that human beings would not naturally ingest – any more than they would drink paint-stripper. If we have to get rid of sugar, we must find an acceptable natural alternative – and that is what I have sought to do in each of my three books on the subject.

Sugar became an important element in western diets in the mid-nineteenth century when industrialization made it possible to refine large quantities cheaply. Previously it was used sparingly as a condiment and medicine. World annual production in 1800 was 250,000 tonnes; today over 100 million tonnes are produced each year, with a value of more than £11,000 million. In Britain, added sugars account for between 18 and 25 per cent of the calories in a typical diet. The average UK citizen eats 45 kilograms (100 lbs) of sugar each year, a national consumption of almost 1 kg (2 lbs) per person per week.

One third of this is sugar used in the kitchen. Twice as much is consumed, usually unknowingly, in manufactured foods. The existence of these sugars in the foods you buy is not clearly indicated. It is masked under different technical names and infiltrated into the unlikeliest of products. The London Food Commission has discovered that chips prepared at a large burger chain were generously sprinkled with dextrose, a form of sugar. Sugar is used in most ketchups, pickles, sausages, mayonnaise, tinned spaghetti, baked beans, crackers and salted biscuits, baby foods and rusks and breakfast cereals.

Children under eighteen are at greatest risk. They consume one third of all sweets and chocolates sold, in addition to a high proportion of soft drinks and convenience foods. The biscuit and confectionery industries spend £100 million a year on advertising heavily sugared products. Much of the promotion is aimed at children. A survey by the anti-sugar group Action and Information on Sugars found that over half of the advertisements on children's television were for food, and 78 per cent of these were for products high in sugars or fats or both.

Sugar makes you eat more than you need. Compare how you feel after eating an apple (which takes time to chew and digest) with how you feel after drinking a cup of tea sweetened with a heaped teaspoon of sugar. The sweet tea still leaves you wanting something more – the apple sates your hunger. If you ate two apples and compared it to drinking one cup of tea sweetened with two generous teaspoons of sugar the difference would be even more marked. Sugar is such a refined food that although it contains the same amount of carbohydrate as the apples, the stomach does not feel full and demands more. The result is overeating. And overeating makes you overweight. As an overweight person you are a prime candidate for the twentieth-century killer diseases – coronary heart disease, cancer, diabetes, stroke, gallstones and kidney stones. In Britain the proportion of people who are over-weight has risen from one third in 1980 to over 40 per cent today. Glasgow has been designated 'coronary capital of the world'.

Dental caries costs the NHS in excess of £1 billion a year. Nearly half the nation's under-fives suffer from some tooth decay, and every working day in England and Wales ninety children under the age of five undergo a general anaesthetic for teeth to be extracted. 'The problem is not sugar,' claims Neil Shaw, the chairman of sugar manufacturers Tate and Lyle. 'In this country 10 per cent of people do not have a toothbrush.'

Against the mounting volume of evidence the sugar industry is spending £12 million in a three-year campaign to depict sugar as natural and safe. Television images of plants, birds and insects deliver a dubious contention that sugar has been part of our lives since the beginning of time. 'Sugar is a grass, a very natural food . . . People need to understand that sugar is natural part of the diet,' says the chairman of Tate and Lyle.

Dr W. K. Heaton of the University of Bristol's Department of Medicine disagrees. Sugars, he says, are essentially food additives or artificial sweeteners. If they were sub-jected to the same tests as new additives 'they would fail all of them'.

The Sugar Bureau, public face of the UK refining industry (dominated by Tate and Lyle and British Sugar), has distributed a seventy-five-page *Science and Technology for Seasonal Celebrations* pack to 24,000 primary schools around the country, promoting pseudo-scientific experiments with household sugar. Children are encouraged to add sugar to drinks until they 'taste right'. There is, understandably, no mention of any dental or general health risks. Some of the information aimed to help 'understand the meaning and importance of a balanced diet' is deliberately misleading on scientific grounds and contravenes current health policy. In one activity children are told to brush their teeth, chew a sweet and then use a disclosing tablet, which would show no residue of plaque, implicitly exculpating sugar from dental decay. The risk of decay, of course, stems from long-term building-up of plaque rather than in fairground tricks of this kind.

The manufacturers of Ribena, the drink with fifteen lumps of sugar in each small carton, have also turned their attention to schoolchildren. Free cases of Ribena were sent to schools for Christmas parties in 1991, and 2,000 schools were targeted to receive free crates for summer fêtes. Free offers like these pave the path to the dentist's chair.

'The sugars in an apple are no different from the sugars in a chocolate bar,' claims a Sugar Bureau spokesperson. In fact the government's report on *Dietary Sugars and Human Disease* (1989) distinguished clearly between these two types of sugars. The sugar in an apple was called intrinsic sugar – wrapped in fibrous plant cells. The sugars used to sweeten chocolate were defined as non-milk extrinsic sugars – extracted from their plants cells and no longer part of a cellular structure. These are generally known as 'added sugars'. It is added sugars that are indicted as the main cause of tooth decay, not sugars that are naturally present in food.

In the heat of debate one group and condition is overlooked. Diabetes among children under fifteen has doubled since 1977. This year, another 13.5 children in 100,000 will be afflicted by this disruptive, pervasive and life-shortening disease. The number is rising all the time and for no obvious reason.

Diabetes is described as a controllable condition. Inject the right amounts of insulin and eat a balanced diet and, all being well, there will not be too many dangerous attacks of hyperglycaemia or hypoglycaemia. Adults can just about cope with the regime. Children face, in addition to the medical regime, an acute social problem. It is excruciating for a child at any age to stand out from the crowd. A diabetic child generally conceals the private world of injections, eating habits and various other precautions from his or her friends.

In one aspect, however, the child is glaringly exposed, separated from society by a cruel intervention. Children today are bombarded from morning to night by sugar propaganda. In every commercial break on children's television one in two jingles will promote a sugar product. Chocolate bars blare from hoardings on every street corner. There are sweets ranged intentionally at children's eye level at supermarket check-outs. Even comics come with free sweets attached. Lessons at school have been infiltrated by sugar propagandists. The child with diabetes lives with a painful dilemma: either eat poison to stay with the crowd, or risk social isolation. Some manage to balance moderate sweet-eating with sociability, but miscalculation is easy and the risks are considerable. Their sense of deprivation, material and social, is indescribable.

In the campaign against sugar, no one speaks for these children, whose numbers are growing year by year and who deserve to be protected from unnecessary pain. Packs promoting sugar must be banned from schools. Restrictions should be placed on television advertising, removing the promotion of sugar-risk products beyond the 9 p.m. bench-mark. It is high time for the government to take action, both to protect the next generation and to shield those whose lives can be shortened by sugar.

'Cut out sugar' – it's official

Government reports on sugars have developed an increasingly tighter line in recent years in their attitude towards sugars and their place in our diet. The 1989 Committee on Medical Aspects of Food Policy (COMA) report on *The Role of Dietary Sugar in Human Disease* unequivocally called for 'the reduction of non-milk extrinsic sugars' as 'part of the general reduction in dietary energy intake'. Initially reluctant to recommend levels of sugar consumption, by 1991 the committee in the COMA report on *Dietary Reference Values for Food Energy* stipulated a maximum individual intake of added sugars at 10 per cent of the average diet – half the actual amount eaten. Any more than twelve teaspoons (60 g) per day was likely to endanger health.

The World Health Organization, in a 1990 report on *Diet, Nutrition and the Prevention of Chronic Diseases*, went so far as to say that the best solution was to eat no sugar at all. It ruled that between 0 and 10 per cent of total calorie consumption represented the desirable range of intake for 'free sugars' – that is, refined or added sugars. Professor W. P. T. James, who chaired the report, wrote in a letter to the author: 'There is very little evidence, if any, that one actually needs refined sugars in the diet.' His report emphasized the links between sugars and dental caries, and pointed out that sugars provide no nutritional benefit and displace healthy foods that are rich in minerals and vitamins.

In 1991 the UK Health Education Authority produced a popular illustrated booklet, *Enjoy Healthy Eating*, which put across its simple message in words and pictures. A downcast face made up of chocolate biscuits, jam cream cakes and sweets is contrasted with a cheerful one with a watermelon mouth and kiwi eyes. The text is concise and to the point: 'Sugar contains only calories with no other nutrients. You do not need sugar for energy.'

There are signs that the food industry has begun to take note. Heinz has cut sugar by 22 per cent in its baked beans over the last eight years, a kind of health education by stealth. This still leaves them in seventh place compared to other baked bean manufacturers: six out of nine brands tested by the *Food Magazine* contained less sugar. Waitrose sweeten their baked beans with apple juice instead of sugar. Most supermarket chains and manufacturers produce tinned fruit in apple or pear juice as an alternative to heavy syrups. Sugar-free and sugar-reduced jam have become widely obtainable. On the other hand, Coca Cola still sponsor the Olympics, Mars bars run with the London Marathon and the decathlete Daley Thompson peddles a glucose drink that is supposed to promote sporting energy. There is still some way to go before the world acknowledges that sugar is not only worthless but harmful.

Artificial Sweeteners

Artificial non-sugar sweeteners have been around since the nineteenth century, and questions about their safety were raised almost from the outset. A perceptible switch towards sweeteners was evident in the last third of the present century, when slimness was idealized and people became aware that sugar made them bulge in the wrong places. The world market for artificial sweeteners is worth vast sums of money, most of which is spent in the United States.

The food industry, whose priorities are durability and low cost, adopted artificial sweeteners in tandem with high-sugar products. Coca Cola has the equivalent of seven teaspoons of sugar in a small can and as much aspartame in the Diet version. Many orange squashes mix sugar and artificial sweeteners. Products for the diabetic market are almost uniformly reliant on non-sugar sweeteners, sometimes warning of the risk of over-indulgence.

Aspartame, marketed as Nutrasweet until the end of 1992, was passed for use in fizzy soft drinks by the American Food and Drug Administration in 1983. In 1990 it was under review by the British government's Committee on Toxicity, following evidence presented by Dr Erik Millstone of Sussex University. In the United States, consumers and groups such as Aspartame Victims and Their Friends have called for aspartame to be more rigorously tested as a drug, rather than as a food additive. Dr. H. J. Roberts, author of *Aspartame (Nutrasweet): Is it Safe?* (Charles Press, 1990), began a private investigation when a patient came to him suffering from seizures as a result of severe hypoglycaemia and he reports that abstention from aspartame prevented any further low blood-sugar seizures. The product remains a widely used alternative to sugar, although the UK government has issued warnings about its use by sufferers from phenylketonuria, an inborn defect of protein metabolism.

Anything sweetened with **saccharin** is required in the United States to carry a health label warning that it can cause cancer in laboratory animals. Saccharin was invented in 1879 and has been banned at various times and in various countries. It is currently off the shelves in Canada but is used extensively in Britain in soft drinks, ice lollies and pickles. Diabetics consume more saccharin than the rest of the population and have been advised by the Ministry of Agriculture, Fisheries and Food to avoid exceeding a maximum daily intake of 5 mg per kilo of body weight. Saccharin is also used to sweeten medicine and vitamins, though UK food regulations specify that it may not be used in baby foods.

Sorbitol is used in ice cream, confectionery, chewing

gum, soft drinks, medicine and in foods intended for diabetics. There is some evidence that high doses contribute to the formation of bladder tumours in laboratory rats. Even moderate consumption can provoke diarrhoea.

Quite apart from questionable safety, there is clear evidence that some artificial sweeteners may increase the appetite. Artificial sweeteners, according to Dr John Blundell of Leeds University, 'actually prompt hunger or promote a liking for the calories which the body is deprived of while it is consuming an artificial sweetener'. The artificial sweetener may add on its own hunger or it may leave dieters with a residual hunger which they don't expect to have. Blundell and his colleague Dr Rogers have published an important paper on the different effects of saccharin and carbohydrates on hunger. The effect of a sweet taste on the human palate stimulates the appetite, no matter whether the origin is sugar or artificial sweetener. Instead of helping you cut down sugar, they make you eat more than usual and consequently get fatter and feel unwell. They have no place in a healthy lifestyle, and I have excluded them from all my recipes.

The only way to eliminate sugar is with sweetness provided by nature. Honey must be avoided since, like sugar, it contains no fibre and very few nutrients. Fructose, commercially prepared fruit sugar, is twice as sweet as sugar. At one time it was considered suitable for diabetics, but it is now not thought to offer any advantage over sugar. That leaves fruit and its juices as the only natural way to stay sweet and healthy.

The Fruit Route

What you get in a fruit, any fruit, is a complex, completely satisfying food rich in fibre, vitamins, minerals and even protein. Fruit is not invariably cheap but it is filling and it keeps you going for hours. When Moses sent scouts to the Promised Land they returned not with gold and silver but with bowers laden with fruit.

FRESH FRUIT

All fresh fruit is sweet, but while all taste best eaten raw some lend themselves well to baking in an oven.

Apples – I use eating apples rather than cooking apples, which are sour tasting. The number of varieties available in the shops is on the increase and apart from the ubiquitous Golden Delicious it is possible to find Coxes, Spartans and Jonathans in season.

Pears – Two common varieties seen in the shops are Conference, which are long and thick skinned, and Comice, which tend to be squatter with a thin skin. Pears are usually hard when sold and ripen at home when stored in a cool cupboard. If you don't want them to soften, store in the fridge. They are sweeter and moister than apples and are often used in combination with them in these recipes.

Bananas – Mashed into a purée they give a light sponge texture to cakes, even sufficient to roll them into roulades. They are also excellent as a sweetening agent; the amount used is critical, however – too much and the banana flavour dominates! The weights in all the recipes are *without* the peel. Use bananas when they are yellow and ripe, but not so ripe that they are soft and oozing out of their skins. Store in a cool dark cupboard rather than the fridge, which will make them soggy and black skinned.

Fresh dates – These are very sweet: three dates weighing

about 50 grams (2 oz) are equivalent to 10 grams carbohydrates (CHO). When used to sweeten cakes, they give
a moist, succulent flavour, and they can also be mixed
with chopped nuts to make sweetmeats. There are two
types of dates available in the shops: long, smooth-
skinned ones imported frozen from Israel and round,
plump, crinkly-skinned dates costing roughly twice as
much from California.

Pineapples, *gooseberries* and *blackberries* go well in crumbles
and pies but should be mixed with apples or pears to lower
their acid taste.

Peaches, *nectarines*, *strawberries* and *raspberries* have delicate flavours that are spoilt by cooking.

Oranges and *lemons* – The perfumed skins of these citrus
fruits may be finely grated and added to cakes and puddings for extra flavour. The residues from post-harvest
treatments given to oranges and lemons to prolong their
shelf-life cannot be removed by washing. In Germany and
France the fruits are stamped with a warning notice, but
there is no indication in this country. The way to avoid the
residues is to buy unwaxed or organic fruit. This is particularly important in recipes like Lemon Tart, where you eat
the grated skin. In the UK two supermarket chains,
Waitrose and Safeways, regularly stock organic produce,
but you may find cheaper fruit at health-food stores and
specialized greengrocers.

DRIED FRUITS

These are high in carbohydrates but you need less for a
recipe than the equivalent amount of sugar. Dried fruits
have half as many calories as sugar and are high in fibre and
minerals.

They provide a deep, sweet taste in cakes. *Raisins* and
sultanas can be used whole. *Dried dates*, containing 8.7
grams fibre per 100 grams, blend easily into a mass when

heated in water; after a few minutes of simmering in a little water, they can be mashed to a paste with a fork.

Raisins are small dried grapes containing 6.8 grams fibre per 100 grams and can be used as an alternative to dates. If a paste is specified in a recipe they should be blended in an electric coffee grinder or small food processor.

Dried apricots and *prunes*, with their distinctive flavours, contain less carbohydrates than the previous three dried fruits – 25 grams is equivalent to 10 g CHO (carbohydrate). Dried apricots are bright orange in colour if preserved with sulphur and dark brown if not. The hunza apricot is a variety of hard dried apricot which has to be soaked for a number of hours before it becomes soft enough to eat.

Dried figs are high in fibre – 18.5 grams per 100 grams. Turkey provides the largest supply of figs. In this book I have used them to sweeten pastry, first grinding them finely in a food processor. I do not presoak them – this would make the pastry overly moist.

Dried peaches and *apple rings* are harder to find in the shops but are delicious in fruit salads or as a nibble.

Using fresh and dried fruit as a sweetener in three books has meant constant experimenting to achieve results that are delicate and sweet. I have included some favourite recipes that I wanted to convert to sugar-free versions for many years but had to wait until I had greater knowledge about the chemistry of the different ingredients and their interaction.

FRUIT JUICE

Fruit juice provides vitamins and minerals but no fibre, and I use it in small amounts in some recipes. If drunk neat, it sends blood sugar levels soaring; this does not occur in these recipes because the juice is mixed with other fibrous ingredients.

Ideally, squeeze your own juice. It tastes best, and you know it has not been diluted or adulterated. When buying packets of juice, study the ingredients. Anything described as a 'Juice Drink' should be avoided. It is quite legal for a drink with this description to contain 95 per cent water, 5 per cent juice and up to fifty lumps of sugar per litre. (Even products sold as 'Hi-juice' can contain as low an amount of juice as 20 per cent.)

'*Pure Juice*' is made of imported concentrated juice which is transported in tankers and has water added before packaging. Packets bear the label 'unsweetened' but the Ministry of Agriculture discovered, while researching the different substances found in twenty-one brands of orange juice in 1991, that Safeways and Sainsburys Pure Juice had a fifth of its sugar content from sugar beet, as also did St Michael's Jaffa Juice. (Many also included more than one third pulpwash – pulpwash is produced by soaking the left-over squeezed oranges in water and squeezing them again.)

When the juice is reconstituted, extra water is sometimes added to make it go further but this weakens the taste so sugar, citric acids and flavourings are used to restore the original taste. Food regulations allow up to 1.5 per cent sugar to be added to juice before it has to be described as sweetened.

As a result of the Ministry of Agriculture investigation of juices, prosecutions under the Trades Description Act and the Food Safety Act were prepared against eleven super-markets and fruit juice manufacturers for allegedly mis-leading consumers over 'pure' and 'unsweetened' orange juice. The orange juices that used no beet sugar, corn syrup or pulpwash were Del Monte pure juice, De L'Ora pure juice, St Ivel real juice, Waitrose pure juice and Tesco pure juice.

Giving Up Sugar

Giving up something you are used to is hard, and with a pervasive substance like sugar it is even harder. The long-established habit of eating unnaturally sweetened food is difficult to dispense with in a day. And even after making the decision to give up, staying off requires a conscious recognition of the benefits brought by a sugar-free life. You know the risks involved in sugar consumption; by eliminating sugar you lengthen your life expectancy as dramatically as you would by giving up cigarettes, drugs and unsafe sex. As with weaning from the weed, there are certain immediate boons. You will lose weight in weeks, have a steadier blood-sugar count and feel fitter and more equable. No more irritability caused by low blood-sugar if a snack is a few minutes later than usual. Bulky *Roseanne* comedienne Roseanne Arnold announced 'I ain't going to starve' when she foreswore sugar in a bid to lose weight for her second marriage. She shed three stone in the early stages and 60 lb in three years. 'I'm clean, sober, thinner and happy in love,' she tells reporters.

'But what do I do about sugar in tea?' That's basic, and insoluble by substitutes. Cut your normal sugar ration in half the first fortnight, half again the second; re-educate your taste buds. Eliminate altogether in a month. It helps to eat a sugar-free biscuit while drinking the tea. Expect to modify your eating habits rather than rush headlong into dramatic changes. If you force yourself not to eat something you will feel resentful and vulnerable to temptations.

Don't impose a food dictatorship on yourself. Sweet foods are given as rewards or comfort in our culture and you must avoid punishing yourself by withholding these pleasures. Eat as many cakes and sweets and desserts as you fancy – provided they are sugar-free and fibre-rich. Enjoy the lightness of fruit-flavoured cakes and desserts. As your

repertoire of non-sugar recipes increases you will observe
the way that sugar masks other ingredients. You will
rediscover the real taste of fruit, just as smokers regain their
senses of taste and smell. Carrots, even onions, begin to
taste sweet – carrot juice can be marvellously refreshing.

The pace of change differs with every individual – don't try to
force or hurry it. Some people hardly notice the loss, others
find it physically painful. Dr Robert Lefever, who works
with people suffering from serious eating disorders,
observes that when his patients give up sugar and white
flour 'there is a ten-day withdrawal period during which
people feel irritable and dizzy and may suffer from head-
aches. Clinically there is no doubt that those of us who have
eating disorders find that sugar and white flour are the
substances that make us crave.'

Your *environment* at home, work and school makes a huge
difference. If people around you are fairly health conscious
they are likely to be supportive; gorgers may mock and
place temptation in your path. Try to think how much
better you will feel at the end of the day, and the end of the
year.

SOME TIPS

- Take alternative snacks in your pocket, briefcase, hand-
  bag or back-pack. Fruit bars and strips of dried fruit
  purée will give you a concentrated burst of energy when
  needed. Sugar-free biscuits will provide slow-burning
  energy. Beware of healthy-looking cereal bars; they are
  often high in added sugars.
- Spread your bread with sugar-free jam or, as it is legally
  known, pure fruit spread.
- End your meals with fresh fruit, fruit-filled pies or
  compotes.
- Buy tinned fruit in fruit juice, not heavy syrups. Read the
  labels carefully.

- Avoid 'diet' drinks – they are highly sweetened and don't help change your taste sensitivity. Aim to use freshly squeezed juice diluted to taste.

At the supermarket:

- Look for baked beans and breakfast cereals with no added sugar.
- Forget fruit yogurts, which are sweetened either with sugar or artificial sweetener; make your own.
- Anything on a label ending in '-ose' – sucrose, glucose, dextrose, fructose, maltose – is sugar in disguise, as are 'invert syrups' or 'hydrogenated glucose'. Also watch out for outrageous 'sugar-free sweets' that contain some form of sugar if artificial sweeteners have not been used.
- Beware the word 'natural', one of the most abused of all advertising terms. One particular 'natural' fizzy orange drink on sale in a health-food chain has sugar listed as its second largest ingredient.

Many people go out of their way to avoid eating white sugar but still consume huge amounts of brown sugar or honey. Look at the following figures to give yourself a clearer idea of what every 100 grams (4 oz) of each of the different sweeteners give you.

Figures for muscavado sugar and raw cane sugar are not yet available from the Ministry of Agriculture or the US Department of Agriculture. It is possible to estimate that if muscavado sugar has a range of 84–89 per cent white sugar the remainder consists of moisture, impurities and molasses. The molasses will provide some minerals but because only a small percentage is used with white cane or beet sugar they provide considerably less minerals than 100 grams of dried fruit.

Sweeteners: How They Compare

	SUGAR CONTENT	FIBRE	CALORIES
White sugar	99.9 g	0 g	394
Demarara	99.3 g	0 g	394
Honey	76.4 g	0 g	288
Bananas (without peel)	23.2 g	3.4 g	95
Dried dates	63.9 g	8.7 g	248
Raisins	64.4 g	6.8 g	246
Sultanas	64.7 g	7.0 g	250
Dried figs	52.9 g	18.5 g	213
Prunes	40.3 g	16.1 g	161
Dried apricots	43.4 g	24.0 g	182

Source: McCance and Widdowson, *The Composition of Foods*,
HMSO

High Fibre and Low Fat

High fibre and low fat are the cornerstones that these recipes are based on. The recipes all comply with the recommendations of the WHO report on *Diet, Nutrition and the Prevention of Chronic Diseases* (1990) and the British government's COMA report on *Dietary Reference Values for Food and Energy* (1991). Both reports urge an increase in our diet in the amount of complex carbohydrates – such as wholewheat flour, pulses and beans – and a reduction in the amount of fat, especially fats of animal origin such as lard, dripping, cream and cheese. The recipes in this book follow these guidelines. Only complex carbohydrates such as wholewheat flour, oats and brown rice are used. The advantage of using flour ground from the whole grain is that it contains B-vitamins and essential minerals that are largely removed in the white refined version. Wholewheat flour is used in such a way that the desserts are light and delicate, not solid wedges of stodge.

Fat, when it is used, is always in lower amounts than

usual. Skimmed milk is preferred to full fat milk. Yogurt and fromage frais are used in preference to cream with its notorious high fat content. I also use tofu as a dairy-free cream. It is made from soy bean curd and is low in fat and calories but high in protein. Originally from China and Japan, it is growing in popularity in the West. The type used in the recipes is fresh firm tofu, which is available from health food shops or – fresher and more cheaply – from specialist Chinese, Japanese and Malaysian grocers.

The type of ingredients used in this book result in a more highly defined taste. The recipes do not just substitute wholewheat flour for white and fruit for sugar but represent a new and revolutionary way of making sweet dishes that takes into account taste, texture and health.

Measurements

Measurements are given throughout in both metric (grams) and imperial (ounces) weights, but I would advise you to use metric throughout because these measurements were used when the recipes were created. Also, it is difficult to give exact conversions, and grams are more specific for small quantities: the difference between 25 and 30 grams, for example, is too small to be marked on imperial cooking measures.

Hot Desserts and Puddings

Give me some flour and give me some milk
and we'll have a pudding in half an hour.
Eighteenth-century nursery rhyme

The ingredients have not changed a great deal since the eighteenth century when this nursery rhyme was written. Today we would add an egg and some fruit and might call it clafoutis or cobbler.

Pineapple Crumble

This is a very light crumble.

100 g (4 oz) wholewheat
  flour
25 g (1 oz) sesame seeds
25 g (1 oz) ground almonds
50 g (2 oz) wholewheat
  semolina
1 tsp mixed spice
50 ml (2 fl oz) oil
150 g (5 oz) pear, coarsely
  grated

Filling
300 g (11 oz) fresh pine-
  apple, without skin,
  thinly sliced
100 ml (4 fl oz) unsweet-
  ened pineapple juice
500 g (1 lb 2 oz) eating
  apples, grated

Wash the sesame seeds and dry them.
  Mix the flour, sesame seeds, ground almonds, semolina

and spice together. Stir in the oil and coarsely grated pear. The mixture should form thick crumbs around the pieces of pear.

Use a 20 × 25 cm (8 × 10 inch) baking dish and mix in it the grated apple, juice and thinly sliced pieces of pineapple. Pour the crumble mixture evenly over the top.

Bake in a preheated oven (gas 5/375°F/190°C) for 25–35 minutes, until browned all over.

Makes 8 large portions. Each portion is 25 g CHO. 195 kcals.

Plum and Apple Crumble

Red plums give this crumble a tart taste while Victoria plums provide a less distinctive but sweeter flavour.

Crumble
100 g (4 oz) wholewheat flour
50 g (2 oz) oat bran
25 g (1 oz) porridge oats
25 g (1 oz) desiccated coconut
1 tsp mixed spice
50 g (2 oz) margarine or butter

1 large ripe pear weighing about 150 g (5 oz), grated

Filling
450 g (1 lb) plums
100 ml (4 fl oz) unsweetened apple juice
250 g (9 oz) eating apple, grated

Wash and slice the plums and put them in a saucepan with the apple juice and simmer until they are softened. Remove from the heat and stir in the grated apple. Place in the bottom of a 20 cm (8 inch) diameter baking dish.

Prepare the topping by combining the flour, oat bran, oats, coconut and spice and cutting in the margarine. Rub into crumbs and stir in the grated pear to make a thicker crumbed mixture. Spread this over the top of the fruit and bake in a preheated oven (gas 5/375°F/190°C) for 30 minutes until the crumble is a golden brown and the juice from the fruit bubbles over the crumble topping at the sides.

Serve hot or cold with Banana Ice Cream (page 91).

Makes 16 small portions. Each portion is 125 g CHO. 90 kcals.

Fruit Soufflé

This simple-to-prepare recipe looks very impressive when put on the table. The fluffy soufflé topping contrasts well with the hot fruit in its pink juice. Soufflés are best served immediately after they are removed from the oven – leave them too long and they collapse. The fruit base can be prepared in advance and the soufflé topping whisked up before the start of the meal and put in the oven.

Fruit base
2 ripe peaches weighing about 300 g (11 oz)
225 g (8 oz) strawberries
2 ripe pears weighing about 300 g (11 oz)
2 tbs freshly squeezed or unsweetened orange juice

Soufflé
3 eggs, separated
75 g (3 oz) peeled ripe banana
2 tbs low-fat natural yogurt

Use a deep, 17.5 cm (7 inch) diameter soufflé dish. Depending on the depth of the soufflé dish it may be necessary to tie a collar of greaseproof paper around the top.

Peel the peaches and chop them. Wash and hull the strawberries and slice them thinly. Wash the pears and peel only blemished parts of the skin before dicing. Mix the fruit in the soufflé dish together with the orange juice.

Place the fruit in a moderately hot oven (gas 5/375°F/ 190°C) for 10 minutes to allow the dish and the fruit to become warm.

Prepare the soufflé by either sieving the banana or putting it through a food mill to make a fine purée. Whisk the egg yolks until they are a creamy yellow. Whisk in the banana purée for a few seconds. Fold in the yogurt. Whisk the egg whites until they form stiff peaks. Add half the egg white mixture at a time, stirring as little as possible. Pour this over the fruit and return to a slightly warmer oven (gas 6/400°F/200°C) for 25–30 minutes, until it is well risen and brown. If greaseproof paper has been used remove it and serve the soufflé at once.

Makes 6 portions. Each portion is 12.5 g CHO. 10 kcals.

Carob Soufflé

25 g (1 oz) margarine or butter

25 g (1 oz) wholewheat flour

250 ml (9 fl oz) skimmed milk

75 g (3 oz) carob bar, broken in pieces

50 ml (2 fl oz) unsweetened orange juice

1 dessertspoon Grand Marnier (optional)

2 eggs, separated

desiccated coconut

Melt the margarine in a heavy-based saucepan and stir in the flour with a wooden spoon until a thick ball is formed. Slowly stir in the milk which has been warmed in a separate pan. The flour and fat paste gradually expands and when all the milk has been poured in it will become quite liquid. It is important to add the milk stage by stage so as to avoid lumps.

Melt the carob pieces and orange juice in a bowl placed in a shallow pan of boiling water, or in a double boiler. Add this to the milk sauce and continue to stir gently over a low heat until it thickens. Remove the carob sauce from the heat to cool.

Beat the egg yolks with a fork and gradually add them to the carob mixture together with the liqueur. Whisk the egg whites stiffly and fold them in.

Pour the mixture into a greased soufflé dish. Bake in a preheated oven (gas 5/375°F/190°C) for 25–35 minutes, until the soufflé has puffed up and is firm on top. As you divide the hot soufflé into portions sprinkle some desiccated coconut on top.

Makes 6 portions. Each portion is 10 g CHO. 160 kcals.

Pear Meringue

A flour-free dessert that is light and quick to prepare.

550 g (1 lb 4 oz) pears
50 g (2 oz) ground almonds
50 g (2 oz) almond flakes
½ tsp mixed spice

100 g (4 oz) peeled ripe banana
2 egg whites
50 g (2 oz) desiccated coconut

Wash the pears and grate them coarsely. Stir in the ground and flaked almonds and mixed spice and pour into a 20 cm (8 inch) diameter baking dish.

Sieve the bananas or put them through a food mill. Whisk the egg whites stiffly and gently stir in the liquid bananas. Spread the topping evenly over the fruit and nut mixture. Bake in a preheated oven (gas 2/300°F/160°C) on a low shelf for 30 minutes, until the surface just begins to streak with brown. Sprinkle coconut all over the top and serve. This meringue can also be served cold. Store it in the fridge for up to two days.

Makes 8 portions. Each portion is 7.5 g CHO. 135 kcals.

Cherry Clafoutis

This wonderfully moist cherry dish is well worth making during the short summer season.

450 g (1 lb) black cherries
2 tbs unsweetened apple
   juice
2 eggs
150 g (5 oz) peeled ripe
   banana

60 g (2 oz generous)
   wholewheat flour
½ tsp vanilla essence
225 ml (8 fl oz) skimmed
   milk

Wash and dry the cherries. Remove the stones and place the cherries around the base of a 20 cm (8 inch) diameter baking dish. Sprinkle the apple juice over them.

Whisk the eggs well. Convert the banana to a smooth liquid by putting it through a sieve or a food mill and whisk into the eggs. Stir in the flour and vanilla essence. Gradually add the milk.

Pour the batter over the cherries and bake in a preheated oven (gas 5/375°F/190°C). Cook for 35–45 minutes until the cherry juices come bubbling over the browned sides – a knife plunged into the middle should come out cleanly. This dessert tastes best served hot and because of that there is no need to grease the baking dish if you serve the clafoutis straight from it.

Makes 12 portions. Each portion is 10 g CHO. 60 kcals.

Apple Pudding

'An apple a day keeps the doctor away' probably refers to the vitamin C found in apples. The amount of vitamin C varies from 5 to 30 mg depending on the variety of apple and on the amount of time they have been stored. After several months storage there is as much as 50 per cent loss of vitamin C, although the minerals will remain intact. For a guaranteed daily dose of vitamin C pick your apple straight from the garden tree!

100 g (4 oz) raisins
150 ml (5 fl oz) water
375 g (13 oz) eating apple, grated
25 g (1 oz) unsweetened desiccated coconut

75 g (3 oz) ground almonds
1½ tsp mixed spice
40 g (1½ oz) porridge oats
2 eggs

Grease a 22.5 cm (9 inch) diameter shallow baking dish and preheat the oven (gas 5/375°F/190°C).

Put the raisins in a small pan with the water and simmer over a low heat until they are softened and the water is reduced to about 100 ml (4 fl oz). Cool.

Combine the grated apple and coconut. Add the ground almonds, mixed spice, porridge oats, cooled raisins and their cooking liquid. Whisk the eggs well and stir in.

Pour the mixture into the prepared dish and bake for 30–40 minutes until the pudding is lightly browned on top and firm to the touch. Serve hot or cold with a fruit coulis or Cinnamon-Banana Cream (page 70).

Makes 8 servings. Each serving is 15 g CHO. 155 kcals.

Cherry and Pear Bread Pudding

Slices of oven-browned bread are softened in a pear sauce with juicy cherries baked in between the layers. This is a quick dessert to fling together. It involves only three tasks: buttering the bread, preparing the pear sauce and slicing the cherries. The last takes the longest so if any helping hands can be enlisted this is the job to delegate.

10 slices of wholemeal bread with the crusts re-moved, weighing 200 g (7 oz)

25–40 g (1–1½ oz) margarine or butter
700 g (1 lb 9 oz) ripe pears
150 ml (5 fl oz) water
450 g (1 lb) cherries

Spread the margarine thinly over the surface of the bread. Place the bread, buttered side up, on a baking sheet in an oven heated to gas 5/375°F/190°C until it becomes crisp and slightly brown. Remove from the oven.

Wash the pears and slice them with their skin into a saucepan. Add the water and bring to the boil. Lower the heat and simmer covered for about 5–10 minutes until the fruit is softened and some juice has been released. When the pears have cooled slightly either put through a sieve, food mill or blender to make a thick sauce.

Wash and dry the cherries and slice into halves.

Assemble the dessert in a 20 cm (8 inch) diameter baking dish. Alternate the cherries and broken up pieces of bread on the base of the dish – there is no need to grease it. Make sure that most of the cherries are covered by pieces of bread. Pour the pear sauce evenly over the top and bake at the same temperature as before for 25–35 minutes until the surface of the bread is a golden brown and the pear sauce has been absorbed. It can be served hot or cold.

Makes 8 large portions. Each portion is 22.5 g CHO. 130 kcals.

Apple and Blackberry Pudding

This is a dessert of contrasts – a hot fruit pudding served with a cold sauce conjured out of the same fruit.

400 g (14 oz) eating apples
200 g (7 oz) blackberries
100 g (4 oz) wholewheat flour
25 g (1 oz) soya flour
½ tsp bicarbonate of soda
2 eggs
150 ml (5 fl oz) skimmed milk

150 g (5 oz) peeled banana

Apple and Blackberry Sauce
200 g (7 oz) blackberries
100 ml (4 fl oz) unsweetened apple juice
250 g (9 oz) eating apple
150 ml (5 fl oz) low-fat natural yogurt

Wash and core the apples. Slice them thinly. Wash and pat dry the blackberries. Leave them to stand on a plate.

Combine the flours and bicarbonate of soda. Make a well in the centre and stir in the two eggs, beating well with a fork or spoon so that the flour is gradually absorbed. This way of mixing avoids a lumpy batter. Gradually stir in the milk. Mash the bananas or put them through a food mill and add to the batter. An alternative method is to put the eggs, milk, banana and flours in a liquidizer.

Add the fruit to the batter and pour it into a shallow, lightly greased 20–22.5 cm (8–9 inch) diameter baking dish. Some of the fruit will only be lightly coated with the batter. Bake in a preheated oven (gas 5/375°F/190°C) for 35–45 minutes, until it is a golden brown on top and the juice from the blackberries has begun to spread up the sides of the baking dish.

While the pudding is baking prepare the sauce. Blend the

blackberries and apple juice in a liquidizer. Add the sliced apple and yogurt and blend again. Sieve and chill in the fridge until ready. Serve the hot pudding with the chilled sauce.

Makes 8 large servings. Each serving with sauce is 25 g CHO. 140 kcals.

Squash Pudding

My mother was mesmerized by the sight of two large, round squashes, weighing well over two pounds each, at her local greengrocer's. She bought one for herself and one for me. I was considering slicing and dipping it in egg and wholewheat flour to make crispy fritters when I remembered reading about squash pudding in American literature. The squash provides a bland background for the spices – it bulks out the pudding, while the carbohydrates and calorie content remain low.

75 g (3 oz) dried apricots, chopped
50 g (2 oz) dried dates, chopped
200 ml (7 fl oz) water
75 g (3 oz) peeled banana
75 g (3 oz) fromage frais
75 g (3 oz) low-fat curd cheese

275 g (10 oz) custard squash
1 egg
50 g (2 oz) wholewheat flour
50 g (2 oz) wholewheat semolina
½ tsp mixed spice

Place the chopped apricots and dates in a medium-sized pan with the water and simmer on a low heat until all the water is absorbed. Blend to make a paste. Cool.

Mash the banana with a fork. Mix in the fromage frais and curd cheese. Stir in the dried fruit paste.

Remove the seeds from the squash – they are quite large – and grate the flesh finely. Add to the other ingredients. Whisk the egg and add to the fruit and vegetable mixture. Stir in the flour, semolina and spice.

Pour the mixture into a greased and floured 20 cm (8 inch) diameter baking dish and bake in a preheated oven (gas 5/ 375°F/190°C) for 30–40 minutes, until the surface is evenly browned. Serve hot.

Makes 6 large portions. Each portion is 22.5 g CHO. 130 kcals.

Fruit Crunch

The secret about seeds is that they are stockpiles of minerals and vitamins. Pumpkin seeds contain zinc and sunflower seeds are high in iron. They are both rich in lineoleic unsaturated fatty acid – this is an essential fatty acid that the body cannot make for itself and therefore has to obtain from food. Apart from using them in this recipe they can either be eaten raw or baked. Sprinkle the sunflower seeds with shoyu soy sauce and put in a moderate oven until browned or sprinkle the pumpkin seeds with salt and bake in a slow oven.

Fruit filling
2 peaches weighing about
   300 g (11 oz)
2 nectarines weighing
   about 250 g (9 oz)
2 eating apples weighing
   about 250 g (9 oz)
150 ml (5 oz) water
juice of half a large orange
2 tsp arrowroot

Crunch
25 g (1 oz) pumpkin seeds
25 g (1 oz) sunflower seeds
25 g (1 oz) walnuts
50 g (2 oz) brown rice
   flakes
½ tsp mixed spice
juice of half a large orange
50 g (2 oz) peeled banana

Wash the fruit and chop into 1.2 cm ($\frac{1}{2}$ inch) pieces and put into a pan with the water. Bring to the boil and simmer for 5 minutes until the fruit is softened. Add the orange juice. Put a tablespoon of the liquid into a small bowl and add the arrowroot. Pour back into the pan and stir over a gentle heat until the liquid thickens. Pour into the base of a 20 cm (8 inch) diameter baking dish.

Roughly chop or grind the pumpkin and sunflower seeds and walnuts. Mash the banana. Stir in the brown rice flakes, mixed spice, orange juice and banana. Spread the crunch evenly over the top of the fruit and bake in a preheated oven (gas 6/400°F/200°C) for 15–20 minutes, until it is browned on top.

An alternative method of presentation is to bake the fruit and crunch topping in 6 small individual containers. Serve hot or cold.

Makes 6 portions. Each portion is 25 g CHO. 165 kcals.

Gooseberry and Apple Turnovers

An old friend of mine is wild about gooseberries and can eat her way through huge bowlfuls. I am not such an avid fan – I find them rather tart – but these turnovers make you want to come back for more.

Gooseberries used to be regarded as having medicinal properties. They were considered to be helpful for curing inflammation and as a way of avoiding the plague. One would prefer not to have to put this to the test. But what is good about them is their low carbohydrate content – you have to eat 300 grams (11 oz) before you clock up 10 grams carbohydrate – and the calories only come to 51!

1 quantity Rough-Puff
   Pastry (page 29)

Filling
450 g (1 lb) gooseberries
250 g (9 oz) eating apple
200 ml (7 fl oz) unsweet-
   ened apple juice

Prepare the pastry and leave to stand in the fridge for 30 minutes.

Wash and top and tail the gooseberries. Put them in a saucepan with the chopped apple and juice. Bring to the boil and simmer on a low heat until the fruit is softened. If the fruit was particularly watery and a great deal of liquid remains in the pan, remove the fruit with a slotted spoon and reduce the liquid by boiling. Return the fruit to the pan and boil for a couple more minutes until the remaining liquid is absorbed.

Roll out the pastry thinly on a lightly floured board. Cut out twelve 12.5 cm (5 inch) diameter circles. Place the circles on an ungreased baking sheet and place a heaped table-spoon of the fruit filling in the middle. Before bringing the sides of the circles together make a paste by mixing a little wholewheat flour with water and spreading it along the outer edge of half the circle. Fold the other half on top and pinch the two sides together. This is a more effective way of sealing the filling than dampening the edge.

Place in a preheated oven (gas 6/400°F/200°C) for 25–35 minutes, until evenly browned. Serve hot or cold.

Makes 12 turnovers. Each turnover is 15 g CHO. 90 kcals.

Apricot-Almond Slice

A delicate apricot-flavoured pastry slice, with a buttercup yellow filling.

1 recipe Rough Puff Pastry
  (page 29)

Filling
150 g (5 oz) firm tofu
250 g (9 oz) dried apricots
100 g (4 oz) ground
  almonds

25 g (1 oz) wholewheat
  semolina
1 egg
½ tsp almond essence
1 egg white, lightly
  whisked
25–50 g (1–2 oz) desiccated
  coconut

Prepare the pastry. Leave to stand for 15–30 minutes.

Mince the tofu finely in a food processor or put through a hand-operated food mill.

Heat the dried apricots in 225 ml (8 fl oz) water until softened and the water is absorbed. Add to the minced tofu in the food processor and blend with the ground almonds, semolina, egg and almond essence. (If making by hand use more water with the dried apricots and cook longer so that they are softer and can more easily be sieved or put through a food mill. Combine with the tofu and dry ingredients. Whisk the egg lightly and fold in.)

Roll out half the pastry into a very thin circle large enough to cover the base and sides of a 22.5 cm (9 inch) diameter baking tin. Pour the apricot filling evenly over the pastry base. Roll out the remaining pastry to make a lid and place on top, pinching together at the sides. Prick the surface with a fork. Bake in a preheated oven (gas 5/375°F/190°C). Remove from the oven after 30 minutes and quickly brush the surface with the lightly whisked egg white. Sprinkle all over with coconut and return to the oven for a further 10 minutes. Serve hot or cold.

Makes 16 large slices. Each slice is 15 g CHO. 155 kcals.

Rice Pudding

A nursery dish that everyone likes. If you serve this to toddlers use ground almonds rather than flaked.

75 g (3 oz) short-grain brown rice	100 g (4 oz) peeled ripe banana
600 ml (1 pt) skimmed milk	50 g (2 oz) sultanas
1 cinnamon stick	50 g (2 oz) flaked almonds

Wash the rice well. Put it in a saucepan with the milk and cinnamon stick. Bring to the boil and cook, covered, on a very low light for one hour. Not all cookers can provide a really low heat but a heat diffuser placed over a gas burner can reduce the heat considerably. After one hour the rice should be soft and a fair amount of the milk will be absorbed. Remove any skin from the surface of the milk and add the mashed banana and sultanas. Continue cooking for a further 20 minutes. Remove from the heat and allow to cool. Remove the cinnamon stick and pour the rice mixture into abowl.

Toast the flaked almonds a golden brown and mix them in with the pudding just before serving. Their crispness provides a pleasing contrast with the soft rice.

Makes 6 portions. Each portion is 25 g CHO. 155 kcals.

Baked Apple

A variation on a popular favourite – instead of stuffing the apple with sultanas try this date and cinnamon-flavoured almond paste.

4 medium-sized eating
apples
30 g (1 oz generous) dried
dates
100 ml (4 fl oz) water
½–1 tsp cinnamon
30 g (1 oz generous)
ground almonds

4 dessertspoons of freshly
squeezed lime juice
4 dessertspoons of un-
sweetened apple juice
1 tbs water

Select unblemished apples because the skin protects the apple flesh while it is cooking. Remove the cores from the apples, making a slightly larger opening at one end of the apple. Place the fruit in a baking dish.

Heat the dates with the water in a small pan until most of the water is absorbed and the dates can be mashed to a liquidy paste with a fork. Remove from the heat. Mix in the combined cinnamon and ground almonds. Spoon the date filling into the centre of each apple – use the handle of the spoon to push down the filling. Spoon a dessertspoon of lime juice and apple juice over each apple. Place a table-spoon of water in the baking dish.

Bake in the bottom part of a preheated oven (gas 4/350°F/ 180°C) for 20–30 minutes, until softened but still firm.

Each apple is 20 g CHO. 120 kcals.

Nectarine Brûlée

Nectarines are similar to peaches. Their flesh is firmer and their skin is smooth rather than velvet. Their carbohydrate value is slightly higher – 12.4 grams per 100 grams compared to peaches which are only 9.1 grams per 100 grams.

450 g (1 lb) nectarines   100 g (4 oz) peeled banana
200 ml (7 fl oz) low-fat
  fromage frais

To grate the nectarines, cut them in half and hold the cut
side against the grater. The skin will protect your fingers.
When you have finished grating, discard the skin. Spoon
the fruit into a 15 cm (6 inch) diameter baking dish. Spread
the fromage frais over the surface of the fruit. Sieve the
banana over as much of the fromage frais as possible and
place under a medium grill. This will heat the nectarine and
lightly brown the banana. Avoid letting the banana over-
brown or the texture becomes hard and tacky.

Makes 4 small portions. Each portion is 17.5 g CHO. 85
kcals.

Apricot Dumplings

This Passover recipe uses ground unleavened bread –
matza meal – as the basic carbohydrate. During Passover,
bread and flour are forbidden and this prohibition has
produced a number of ingenious recipes. The problem with
matza meal is that it reacts on other ingredients as cement
does on bricks – it binds them together in a solid block. Eggs
are used to counter these tendencies.

The advantage of this recipe is that the apricot dumplings
or *knaidlech* can be prepared the day before and kept in the
fridge. The sauce should be prepared the same day and
used to heat the dumplings in.

Matza meal can be purchased in the large supermarket
chains.

2 eggs
2 tbs oil
100–125 ml (4–4½ fl oz)
  warm water
125 g (4½ oz) matza meal
9 plump dried apricots
  weighing 75–90 g (3–3½
  oz)

Apple Sauce
550 g (1 lb 4 oz) eating
  apples
½ tsp ground cinnamon

Whisk the eggs and add the oil and warm water. Fold in the
matza meal and stir – it will thicken up in a couple of
minutes. The mixture will be stiff but not as dry as dough.
Cover and leave in the fridge for at least one hour.

Simmer the apricots in 100 ml (4 fl oz) water until it is
absorbed and the apricots have swelled. Cut each one into
four pieces.

Remove the dumpling mixture from the fridge and,
dipping your hands in cold water, roll into 36 small balls.
Flatten out each ball and place piece of apricot on top and
then fold and roll into a ball again. When they are all
prepared fill a large saucepan with about 10 cm (4 inches)
water and bring to the boil. Drop the balls in and simmer
uncovered for about 15 minutes. As they begin to cook they
will rise to the surface of the water and slowly expand.

Prepare the sauce while the dumplings are cooking.
Wash and slice the apples and simmer in a little water with
the cinnamon until they are softened. Blend.

Serve the purée hot with the apricot dumplings.

Makes 8 portions. Each portion is 20 g CHO. 130 kcals.

Pastry Desserts

'When I feel miserable,' said one of my students, 'I go and make some pastry.' And it is true that making and rolling out pastry is very satisfying.

Pastry-making is a simple skill that anyone can learn and enjoy. It provides a basis for all kinds of tarts, sweet and savoury. Confidence comes with practice, but pastry cannot go terribly wrong. The main dangers with dough are that it can be too moist or too dry. All you need do is add a little more flour or a little more liquid. The one other point to remember is that pastry does not require a great deal of working with your hands – it does not need pummelling into shape like a yeast dough. A lightly floured board stops the pastry sticking and a steady, even rolling-out motion gives the best results. Bake in a moderately hot oven rather than cool, and position on the middle or top shelf.

The pastries in this section are made of wholewheat flour, fat or oil and a binding liquid, either water, milk, yogurt or egg yolk. Egg yolk makes the pastry richer, yogurt compensates for the small amount of fat used. The amount of liquid needed is affected by how finely the flour is milled. You may have to use a smidgeon more or less than specified in the recipes, depending on the type of flour you use.

The fat recommended by dietitians is margarine, and polyunsaturated margarines are widely advocated for health. But manufacturers have produced so many varieties that it is hard to know what one is buying – fat-reduced margarines, mixed-fat spread, reduced-fat spread, low-fat spread and very low-fat spread are just some of the types available. The choice seems so confusing one wonders whether buying butter might not be simpler. It may be worth summarizing the state of play in a combative market sector worth £700 million a year:

The market share of *butter* has slipped from 75 per cent in the early 1970s to just 22 per cent today. It contains saturated animal fats which raise cholesterol levels and increase the risk of heart disease. The advantages of butter are that it has been used for over a thousand years and is neither synthetic or untested. It is very tasty and contains vitamins A and D.

Ghee is clarified butter which means that the milk solids have been removed. This does not alter the amount of saturated fat it contains.

Margarines made with sunflower oil are highest in polyunsaturated fats, and those made with olive oil are highest in monounsaturated fats. They are reinforced with vitamins A and D. They contain the same 82 per cent of fat and 740 calories per 100 grams as butter.

Polyunsaturated margarines made from vegetable oils can contain up to 24 per cent saturated fats; the hardness of the margarine usually betrays the amount of saturated fats used. Margarines that list vegetable oils are not necessarily high in polyunsaturated fats – they can include palm or coconut oil, both of which are high in saturated fat.

Not all margarines rely only on vegetable oils and some are not suitable for vegetarians. According to the official definition of margarine, which was invented in 1869 as a cheap alternative to butter, it must contain not less than 80 per cent animal, fish or vegetable fat.

'Low-fat spreads' are essentially watered down fat. The ratio is usually 40 per cent fat to 55 per cent water and this figure can include saturated fats. This type of margarine contains too much water to be useful in making pastry.

Margarine is made by refining and bleaching oils. It may be flavoured, coloured and mixed with anti-oxidants and emulsifiers. If the margarine is chemically hardened or hydrogenated this creates trans-saturates which are regarded as a possible health hazard.

Reduce! reduce! reduce! – When making pastry, you have to choose between polyunsaturated margarine and butter. Butter gives a pleasing taste but none of my recipes requires enough to affect the taste. Lessen the amount of fat you eat and the butter/margarine discussion becomes less important.

Suggestions for reducing fat in your diet involve cutting back on chips, crisps, biscuits, pies, ice cream, meat and hard yellow cheese. Switching from butter to sunflower margarine reduces blood cholesterol levels but does not begin to tackle the wider problem of high fat consumption. The ultimate alternative is said to be on the drawing board of an American food firm – a totally fat-free spread that will replace margarine and butter. One of the principal ingredients is sugar.

Ingredients and Terms Used in Pastry-Making

WHOLEWHEAT FLOUR – for best results use the finely milled or pastry flour. It is available in specialist health food shops. If you cannot find any, grind ordinary flour finely in a food processor as you need it.

TO BAKE BLIND – this is when pastry is partly or completely cooked before the filling is added. Cover the pastry with greaseproof paper and place dried beans on top. This stops the pastry browning too quickly or puffing up. The beans can be reused.

Sweet Shortcrust Pastry

175 g (6 oz) wholewheat
  flour
25 g (1 oz) ground almonds
65 g (2½ oz) margarine

25 g (1 oz) dried figs
1 egg yolk
100–125 ml (4–4½ fl oz) cold
  water

Combine the flour and ground almonds. Rub in the margarine to make thick crumbs. Use a small food processor or coffee grinder to mince the figs finely, and stir them in. Whisk the egg yolk lightly with a fork and mix with half the water. Stir into the flour mixture, then drizzle in the remaining water as necessary to make very thick crumbs which can be worked by hand into a soft dough. Knead lightly for a minute. Cover with a cloth until ready to use.

Total CHO of the pastry is 130 g. 1280 kcals.

Raspberry Tart

This tart, with its thick lattice-work top, looks attractive on either a dinner table or a hearty farmhouse tea table. The slightly sweetened shortcrust pastry goes very well with the tart taste of the raspberries. For a sweet counterpoint serve with Passion-fruit and Pear Sorbet (page 109).

1 recipe Sweet Shortcrust
  Pastry (above)

Filling
400 g (14 oz) fresh raspberries

100 ml (4 fl oz) unsweet-
  ened apple juice
½ tsp arrowroot
75 g (3 oz) sugar-free raspberry jam
squeeze of lemon juice

Prepare the pastry. Set aside, cover while preparing the filling.

Wash the raspberries and pat them dry with absorbent kitchen paper. Place in a medium-sized saucepan with the apple juice and boil for about 60 seconds. Remove from the pan and put in a bowl to cool.

Roll out just over half of the pastry on a lightly floured board to fit a 20 cm (8 inch) diameter tart dish. Bake blind in a preheated oven (gas 5/375°F/190°C) for 15 minutes, until lightly browned.

When the fruit has cooled pour any juice off the fruit into a small saucepan. Take off a tablespoon of the liquid and mix it with the arrowroot and return to the pan. Bring to the boil and simmer for a minute or two until it thickens. Place the raspberries evenly over the base of the pastry and pour the sauce on top.

The remaining pastry will be used for the lattice topping. Divide into small pieces and roll into 1.25 cm ($\frac{1}{2}$ inch) wide strips. Smooth the sides of the strips with your fingers. Alternate the strips of pastry so that they weave over and under each other. Press the end of the strips firmly against the edge of the partly cooked base. If enough pastry is left over make a final strip around the edge.

Return to the oven (gas 5/375°F/190°C) and bake for 10–20 minutes, until the top of the pastry is browned.

Heat the jam with a tablespoon of water and a squeeze of lemon juice in a pan until melted and sieve over the surface of the tart.

Makes 12 portions. Each portion is 15 g CHO. 125 kcals.

Marzipan Tart

The nuts used in this recipe are good news. A recent report in *Archives on Internal Medicine* based on a study of 34,000 American Seventh Day Adventists (all non-smokers, and about half of whom are vegetarian) found that those who ate a handful of nuts five times a week halved their risk of heart attacks, compared to those who ate them once a week.

No one is sure why nuts protect against heart disease – whether it is the mixture of polyunsaturated and monounsaturated fat, or whether the fibre lowers blood cholesterol (one study has shown this to be the case with almonds), or the rich supply of vitamin E which prevents oxidation of cholesterol. Whatever the reasons are, it makes a welcome change to be urged to eat something rather than cut back. So forget about the expense and try this nutty marzipan tart based on a Portuguese recipe.

1 recipe Sweet Shortcrust
   Pastry (page 22)

Filling
150 g (5 oz) dried figs
125 g (4½ oz) ground almonds

½ tsp almond essence
100 g (4 oz) firm tofu
½ tsp ground aniseed
10 g (½ oz) oats, ground
   into a fine flour
1 egg

Prepare the pastry. Leave to stand for 15–30 minutes.

Heat the figs in a little water until softened and the water is absorbed. Blend in a processor with the ground almonds and almond essence. Mince the tofu through a sieve or food mill and add to the figs. Stir in the ground aniseed and oats. Whisk the egg well and add to the almond mixture.

Roll out half the pastry into a thin circle large enough to cover the base and sides of a 20 cm (8 inch) diameter baking tin. Bake blind in a preheated oven (gas 5/375°F/190°C) for 10–15 minutes, until a delicate biscuit colour.

Pour the marzipan filling into the pastry base. Roll out the remaining pastry to make a lid and place on top. Prick the surface with a fork because the inside will bubble up a little during baking. Bake in a preheated oven (gas 4/350°F/180°C) for 30 minutes.

Makes 16 slices. Each slice is 15 g CHO. 155 kcals.

Shortcrust Pastry

A quick, crispy pastry.

175 g (6 oz) wholewheat
   flour
50 g (2 oz) margarine

1 egg yolk
50–100 ml (2–4 fl oz) water

Cut the margarine up in the flour and rub into crumbs with your fingertips until sandy in texture. Whisk the egg yolk lightly and add half the water. Stir in to the flour and margarine to make thick crumbs. As you stir the crumbs will come together. Bring together with your hands to make a dough, adding more water if necessary. Knead lightly until the pastry is soft to the touch. Leave to stand in a cool place.

Total CHO of the pastry 115 g. 970 kcals.

Sesame-Prune Tart

The prunes and sesame seeds combine to give a mellow melt-in-the-mouth flavour rather like steamed plum puddings and mincemeat tarts.

½ recipe Shortcrust Pastry
   (above)

Filling
50 g (2 oz) sesame seeds
150 g (5 oz) pitted prunes
150 ml (5 fl oz) water
50 ml (2 fl oz) freshly
   squeezed orange juice

1 dessertspoon brandy
   (optional)
½–1 tsp mixed spice
¼ tsp grated orange zest
   (use organic orange)

Topping
1 egg white
75 g (3 oz) peeled banana

Roll out the pastry to fit a 20 cm (8 inch) diameter baking dish and bake blind in a preheated oven (gas 5/375°F/190°C) for 10 minutes, until partially cooked but still pale.

Rinse the sesame seeds well and put in a baking dish in the oven to dry out.

Simmer the prunes in the water until most of the liquid is absorbed. If they are very soft, mash with a fork – otherwise blend in the liquidizer with the orange juice and brandy. Stir in the sesame seeds, mixed spice and orange zest. Spread the prune and sesame mixture over the pastry base and return to the oven for a further 10 minutes.

For the topping, whisk the egg white until it is stiff. Sieve the banana or put it through a food mill so that it is turned into a purée, and stir into the egg white. Spoon this topping evenly over the prunes and return to a lower oven (gas 2/300°F/150°C) for 15–20 minutes, until set and specks of light brown appear on the surface.

Makes 16 small slices. Each slice is 10 g CHO. 70 kcals.

Cherry Tart

This is an adaptation of an Elizabeth David recipe for *Tarte aux Cerises*.

½ recipe Shortcrust Pastry (page 25)

Filling
550 g (1¼ lb) black cherries

50 g (2 oz) sugar-free cherry or plum jam
1 egg yolk
100 g (4 oz) peeled ripe banana, mashed
100 g (4 oz) low-fat yogurt

Roll out the pastry into a circle on a lightly floured board. It should be large enough to cover a 20 cm (8 inch) diameter baking dish. Bake blind in a preheated oven (gas 5/375°F/190°C) for 10 minutes, until a delicate biscuit colour.

Wash the cherries and pat them dry. Remove the stones – there is a special gadget for this purpose sold by hardware and department stores. It is laborious but effective – an ideal job for junior volunteers!

When the pastry case has been removed from the oven, spread the surface evenly with the jam. Lay the cherries on top, packing them tightly as they shrink during cooking.

Whisk the egg yolk. Add the mashed banana and whisk until the mixture is smooth. Fold in the yogurt and pour evenly over the entire surface of the cherries. Their tops will show through the custard. Return the baking dish to the oven and bake for a further 15–20 minutes.

Makes 16 small servings. Each serving is 10 g CHO. 60 kcals.

Lemon Tart

This is based on a recipe by the Roux brothers for that French classic *Tarte au Citron*. My version uses less eggs and, of course, no sugar.

½ recipe Shortcrust Pastry
  (page 25)

Filling
150 g (5 oz) dried dates
200 ml (7 fl oz) water
3 lemons weighing about
  350 g (12 oz)

100 ml (4 fl oz) unsweet-
  ened apple juice
3 large eggs
50 g (2 oz) ground almonds
½ tsp lemon zest (organic
  lemon is best for this)
1 tbsp desiccated cocount

Roll out the pastry on a lightly floured board and place it in a 20 cm (8 inch) diameter baking dish with about 2.5 cm (1 inch) around the sides. Bake blind for 15 minutes in a preheated oven (gas 5/375°F/190°C).

Put the dates in a small saucepan with the water and simmer on a low heat until the water has been absorbed and the dates can be mashed with a fork. Peel the lemons, removing the pith and pips, and place them in a blender with the mashed dates and apple juice and blend well. Whisk the eggs until they are pale and add the ground almonds, lemon zest and lemon and date mixture. The texture of the mixture at this stage is quite runny. Pour into the pastry base.

Bake in a cooler oven (gas 3/325°F/170°C) for 30 minutes. Remove from the oven and sprinkle the surface evenly with the coconut. Return to the oven for a further 10–15 minutes, until the mixture is set firm.

Makes 16 small slices. Each slice is 10 g CHO. 95 kcals.

Prune Tart

½ recipe Shortcrust Pastry
(page 25)

Filling
20 pitted prunes (weighing about 250 g/9 oz)
1 egg

60 g (2 oz generous) peeled banana, mashed or sieved
25 g (1 oz) wholewheat flour
1 tbs armagnac (optional)
100 ml (4 fl oz) skimmed milk

Bring the prunes to the boil and simmer for about 20 minutes until soft and the water is mostly absorbed. They can be prepared the day before, making the dessert simpler to assemble on the day.

Roll out the pastry to fit the base and sides of a 20 cm (8 inch) diameter baking dish. Bake blind in a preheated oven (gas 5/375°F/190°C) for 10–15 minutes, until it becomes a gentle biscuit colour.

Lay out the prunes over the surface of the pastry, packing them fairly close.

Whisk the egg lightly with a fork. Add the banana and continue to whisk for a few minutes longer. Stir in the flour and beat well to remove any lumps. Pour in the armagnac and milk. Pour the mixture over the prunes and pastry base. Return to a cooler oven (gas 4/350°F/180°C) for 20–30 minutes, until browned and firm. Serve hot or warm.

Makes 12 portions. Each portion is 15 g CHO. 95 kcals.

Low-Fat Rough Puff Pastry

This recipe is based on the traditional method used for rough puff pastry but it cuts down the high fat content. It is a supple pastry that can be rolled very thin and gives a light crisp result.

150 g (5 oz) wholewheat   75–100 ml (3–4 fl oz) cold
   flour   water
50 g (2 oz) margarine

Put the flour in a bowl. Add the fat and cut up loosely in the bowl so that it becomes coated with flour. Add enough water to bind the flour and margarine into a soft dough.

Place the pastry on a lightly floured board and roll it out in a narrow oblong about 25 × 7.5 cm (10 × 3 inch). At this stage lumps of fat will be visible in the dough. Mark the pastry off lightly into three sections. Turn the top section over the second and third over on top (see diagram). Give the pastry a quarter turn and repeat the process of rolling out, folding into three and giving a quarter turn three more times. The pastry should then have an even-coloured appearance.

1 Roll out, mark off lightly into three section

2 Fold 1 over 2

3 Fold 3 over 1 and 2

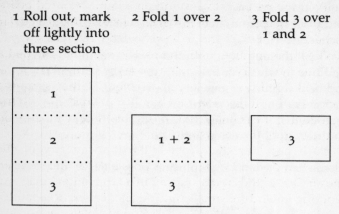

Cover and chill in the fridge for 20 minutes before using.

Total pastry is 100 g CHO. 840 kcals.

Pear Tart

This is an ideal recipe for times when you discover that those iron-hard pears ripened rather quicker than expected and are too soft to serve. They are now perfect to use in this quick recipe which looks rather more fiddly and fancy than it actually is. This tart will keep in the fridge for two to three days, although the pastry is crisper on the first day.

½ recipe Rough-Puff Pastry (page 29)

Filling
1 egg yolk

100 g (4 oz) peeled ripe banana
100 g (4 oz) fromage frais
550 g (1 lb 4 oz) ripe pears

Glaze (optional)
1 tsp lemon juice

50 g (2 oz) sugar-free
plum jam

Roll out the pastry into a round on a lightly floured board and place in a 20–22.5 cm (8–9 inch) tart dish about 4 cm (1½ inches) deep. Bake blind in a preheated oven (gas 5/375°F/190°C) for 15 minutes until the pastry is lightly browned.

While the pastry is baking, prepare the filling. Whisk the egg yolk until it is a pale yellow colour. Either sieve the banana or put it through a food mill and whisk in with the egg. Fold in the fromage frais. Pour this creamy mixture on to the base of the cooked pastry.

Wash and dry the pears and cut away any of the blemished peel. Slice as thinly as possible. Lay the slices on the surface of the cream starting in a large outer circle and working inwards to smaller and smaller circles. Repeat this until all the fruit is used up. Place in a cooler oven (gas 4/350°F/180°C) for 20 minutes, until the base is set.

For the glaze, heat the jam with the lemon juice in a small pan until it has melted and spread this with the back of a spoon over the surface of the cooked pears shortly after removing them from the oven.

Serve cold.

Makes 12 small slices. Each slice is 10 g CHO. 65 kcals.

Yogurt Pastry

This pastry has a cake-like texture. It is not rolled as thinly as rough puff pastry. Yogurt contains more calcium than the equivalent amount of milk and is a healthy food for everyone but especially for women who are concerned to maintain a good intake of calcium and counter osteoporosis. Live yogurt has a less sour taste than low-fat natural yogurt.

150 g (5 oz) wholewheat
   flour
½ tsp bicarbonate of soda
25 g (1 oz) margarine

1 tbs oil
about 90 g (3½ oz) low-fat
   natural or live yogurt

Combine the flour and bicarbonate of soda. Cut the margarine up in the flour and rub into crumbs with your fingertips. Add the oil. Bind with enough yogurt to make a soft flexible dough. Leave to chill for 15–30 minutes before using.

Total pastry carbohydrate 105 g CHO. 840 kcals.

Pear-Fig Tart

This tart comes high on the list of those with the most scrumptious oozing fillings. The sweet fruit filling is balanced by a light pastry and a custard yogurt topping encrusted with almonds.

½ recipe Yogurt Pastry
   (page 31)

Fruit filling
600 g (1 lb 5 oz) ripe pears
75 g (3 oz) dried figs
175 ml (6 fl oz) water
25 g (1 oz) ground almonds
3 drops almond essence or
   1 tbs Calvados

Topping
1 egg
125 g (4½ oz) peeled ripe
   bananas
75 ml (3 fl oz) low-fat
   natural yogurt
40 g (1½ oz) almond flakes
½ tsp ground cinnamon

Prepare the pastry. Leave to stand for 15–30 minutes so that it is easier to handle. Roll out thinly to fit a 25 × 17.5 cm (10 × 7 inch) baking dish. Bake blind in a preheated oven (gas 5/375°F/190°C) for 10–15 minutes until lightly browned.
   Place the figs in a small saucepan with the water and

simmer until most of the water is absorbed. Leave to cool. Wash the pears and slice into the blender. Add the cooled figs. Blend to a thick paste and stir in the ground almonds and almond essence (or Calvados).

Whisk the egg until it is light and frothy. Mash the banana finely until almost liquid and add. Stir in the yogurt.

Combine the almond flakes and cinnamon.

Assemble the tart: pour the fruit filling into the pastry shell and smooth the surface. Spoon the egg and yogurt mixture on top, making the thickness as even as possible. Sprinkle all over with the cinnamon-covered almonds.

Return to slightly cooler oven (gas 4/350°F/180°C) for 30–40 minutes. To test that it is ready put a knife in the middle – it should come out cleanly. Serve cold.

Makes 12 slices. Each slice is 15 g CHO. 110 kcals.

Orange Meringue Tart

The orange custard, sandwiched between a crisp pastry base and soft meringue topping, has a rich sweet taste, almost like a preserve. It is a dish that can be prepared in advance and is guaranteed to make a tremendous impact at a meal.

The recipe uses grated orange rind for extra flavour – try to obtain an organic orange for this purpose because although the thick skin protects the orange flesh from pesticide it cannot be removed from the peel by scrubbing.

½ recipe Yogurt Pastry
  (page 31)

Filling
2 large oranges weighing

about 500 g (1 lb 2 oz)
75 g (3 oz) dried dates,
  finely chopped
2 eggs yolks

25 g (1 oz) wholewheat
   semolina
1 level tsp orange zest

Topping
75 g (3 oz) peeled ripe
   banana
2 egg whites

Prepare the pastry. Cover and put to one side while you make the filling.

Peel the oranges, remove the pips and as much of the white pith as possible. Whizz in a blender for a few seconds until a thick liquid is formed. It should make about 400 ml (14 fl oz) liquid. Pour into a saucepan and simmer with the dates for two to three minutes until they can be mashed with a fork. Remove from the heat.

Lightly whisk the egg yolks with a fork and stir in the semolina and orange zest. Pour the hot juice mixture over the eggs, stirring all the time. Cool.

As the filling cools, roll out the pastry thinly on a floured board to fit a 25 × 17.5 cm (10 × 7 inch) baking dish. Bake blind for 10 minutes, until lightly browned, in a preheated oven (gas 5/375°F/190°C).

Blend the filling once more until it becomes very smooth. Pour into the pastry shell and bake in a preheated oven (gas 4/350°F/180°C) for 15 minutes until the filling has set.

For the topping, sieve the banana or put it through a food mill. Whisk the egg whites stiffly and fold in the liquid banana with a metal spoon. Pour evenly over the entire surface of the firm filling and bake for a further 10–15 minutes in a cooler oven (gas 3/325°F/170°C), until golden brown streaks appear on the surface of the meringue. Serve either hot or cold.

Makes 16 portions. Each one is 10 g CHO. 60 kcals.

Strawberry Shortbread Fingers

The shortbread in this recipe is crisp and sweet. The crispness is a result of combining wheat and rice flours and the sweetness derives from ground dried figs.

Shortbread
65 g (2½ oz) dried figs
100 g (4 oz) wholewheat
    flour
50 g (2 oz) brown rice
    flour

75 g (3 oz) margarine or
    butter

250 g (9 oz) low-fat
    fromage frais
450 g (1 lb) strawberries

Wash and dry the figs and remove the stalks. They should be ground fine – an electric coffee grinder or small processor is best for this. They are not cooked in water first because that would introduce too much liquid into the pastry.

Put the flours, ground figs and fat in one bowl. Cut the fat into small pieces. Rub with your fingers until it forms thick crumbs. Keep on rubbing until the ingredients combine to make a soft pastry. Knead lightly for about 30 seconds until the pastry becomes soft and malleable. Leave covered for 15 minutes. Roll out into a rectangle about 1 cm (½ inch) thick and 7.5 cm (3 inches) wide. Cut into 16 fingers, each one about 7.5 cm (3 inches) long.

Place the shortbread fingers on an ungreased baking tray and prick the surface lightly with a fork. Bake in a preheated oven (gas 3/325°F/170°C) for 25–30 minutes until gently browned.

To assemble, place the shortbread fingers around the sides of an attractive plate, pointing inwards. Spoon half of the fromage frais over the centre of the plate. Hull two-thirds of the strawberries, and place on the fromage frais.

Spoon the remaining fromage frais on top and decorate with the remaining whole strawberries. Leave some with their green leaves on for a colourful effect.

Makes 8 portions. Each portion is 20 g CHO. 175 kcals.

Peach Shortbread Tart

This shortbread tart piled thickly with golden yellow peaches makes a luscious dessert which always disappears very fast. It is best eaten the day it is made but can be stored in the fridge for one more day.

Shortbread crust
65 g (2½ oz) dried figs
100 g (4 oz) wholewheat
   flour
50 g (2 oz) brown rice flour
75 g (3 oz) margarine or
   butter, cut into pieces

Filling
6 peaches weighing about
   900 g (2 lbs)
125 ml (4½ fl oz) unsweetened apple juice
1 tsp arrowroot

Grind the figs finely in an electric coffee grinder or small food processor. They should not be soaked or boiled in water first because it will affect the crispness of the pastry. Combine the flours and add the cut-up margarine and figs. Rub the ingredients together with the tips of your fingers to make thick crumbs. Keep on rubbing a little longer until a pastry is formed. Knead lightly for thirty seconds until the pastry becomes soft and malleable.

Roll out the pastry on a flour-free board. It is very short pastry and you may find it easier to pat it into place directly on the 20 × 25 cm (8 × 10 inch) baking dish, pressing lightly with your fingers to cover the base and sides of the baking dish.

Bake in a preheated oven (gas 3/325°F/170°C) for 20–25

minutes, until the surface is a golden brown and the edges have turned brown. Remove and cool.

Prepare the filling by pouring boiling water over the peaches and leaving to soak for a couple of minutes. Peel and slice thinly. Place them in a saucepan with the apple juice and bring to the boil. Simmer for 2–3 minutes until a little of the juice in the fruit is released, but they should not become soft. Remove with a slotted spoon and place in the pastry shell. Return to the same temperature oven for 5–10 minutes.

Add the arrowroot to a tablespoon of the juice and pour back into the saucepan, stirring until it thickens and the liquid reduces to 4 tablespoons. Leave to cool. Spoon over the cooled fruit to make a thin glaze. The reason for allowing the pastry and fruit to cool between the different stages is to avoid a soggy pastry base.

Makes 10 servings. Each serving is 22.5 g CHO. 150 kcals.

Carob Chip Shortcake with Clementines

150 g (5 oz) wholewheat
  flour
75 g (3 oz) wholegrain
  semolina
100 g (4 oz) margarine
25 g (1 oz) dried dates
60 g (2 oz generous) carob
  drops

1 egg yolk
100–125 ml (4–4½ oz) cold
  water

Topping
300 g (11 oz) clementines
100 g (4 oz) fromage frais
sugar-free plum jam

Combine the flour and semolina. Cut up the margarine into the flour with a knife and rub into thick crumbs. Chop the dates finely in the small cup of a food processor or simmer them with a little water until they can be mashed to a paste with a fork. Stir in the dates and carob drops. If they are large chop them in half so that the carob flavour is well spread through the biscuits.

Whisk the egg yolk and add half the water to it and stir into the flour mixture. Add enough of the remaining water to work the crumbs into a soft dough. Some flours are coarser than others and may require extra water. Leave to rest for about 15 minutes and then roll out to about 1 cm (½ inch) thickness. Cut out 8 rounds of 7.5 cm (3 inch) diameter. Place them on an ungreased baking tray in a preheated oven (gas 4/350°F/180°C) for 20–30 minutes, until they are a gentle biscuit brown. Leave to cool.

Assemble the dessert: peel the clementines and remove any pith. Spread some jam thinly over the surface of each biscuit. Cover with clementine segments and trickle some fromage frais over the top.

Makes 8 portions. Each portion is 25 g CHO. 250 kcals.

Carob Ganache Slices

This is another of those carob desserts that tastes like chocolate.

Three different types of nuts are used in this recipe – almond, hazelnuts and pecans. Pecans are not especially high in protein – they contain 9.2 grams compared to almonds' 21.1 grams. But their oil contains a mixture of monosaturates (60 per cent) and polyunsaturates (25 per cent), while almonds and hazelnuts contain predominantly monosaturated oils. Combining the nuts unites all their different nutritional benefits and makes an elegant and rich dessert.

75 g (3 oz) almonds
75 g (3 oz) hazelnuts
75 g (3 oz) dried dates

150 ml (5 fl oz) water
½ tsp ground cinnamon
2 egg whites

Carob ganache
100 g (4 oz) carob bar
   broken in pieces

150 ml (5 fl oz) low-fat
   yogurt
100 g (4 oz) pecan nuts,
   coarsely chopped

Grind the almonds and hazelnuts to a coarse powder. For a full, deep flavour, cook first in a heavy frying pan over a medium heat without oil, continuously turning them over with a wooden spoon until they become a golden brown. Under, rather than overcook to avoid burning.

Put the dates in a pan with the water and simmer until the water is absorbed and the dates can be mashed with a fork into a paste.

When the date paste and ground nuts have cooled, mix them together with the cinnamon. Whisk the egg whites into stiff peaks and fold them in.

Prepare a 20 × 30 cm (8 × 12 inch) baking tray by greasing the base and covering it with parchment paper. Spread the nut mixture evenly over the base. There should be no holes in the surface. Bake in a preheated oven (gas 3/325°F/170°C) for 20–25 minutes, until firm and very lightly browned. Cool on a wire tray.

Prepare the ganache by melting the carob pieces and yogurt in a bowl over a saucepan of gently bubbling water or in a double boiler. Mix the yogurt and carob together. Remove from the heat and add the chopped pecan nuts.

Cut the nut rectangle in half and spread one side with the cooled ganache. Place the other half on top. Chill in the fridge and just before serving cut into 12 small slices.

Makes 12 slices. Each slice is 10 g CHO. 185 kcals.

Cold Fruit Desserts

Fresh fruit makes the easiest and most effective desserts. The colours are rich and whichever fruit you use the result will catch the eye. Place slices of mango and melon on an attractive china plate with whole strawberries and everyone will coo with pleasure. Or fill wine glasses with segments of clementine and a green grape or two to tantalize appetites.

When fruit is eaten raw it triggers a low insulin response. An experiment measured the different levels of insulin produced by volunteers after eating apples, apple purée and apple juice. Apples yielded a top blood insulin level of 23.9, apple purée 32.3 and apple juice 44.7. The apples were more slowly absorbed because the person eating them has to chew and digest chunks. Purée and juice are broken down before they entered the body, are absorbed quickly and therefore require more insulin to balance the blood sugar level.

There is, of course no need to sprinkle fruit arragements with sugar and there is also no need to pour sauces and alcohol or add spices to 'improve' the flavour. The best way to improve flavour is to use really fresh produce. This section gives ideas for combining fruits and includes basic techniques for stewing. My main aim is to keep the making of recipes simple and to have the results tasting wonderful and looking beautiful.

Basic Fruit Salad

A fruit salad can be made by using whichever fruit is in season. The fruit, if it is large, should be chopped or sliced. Small fruit such as grapes, raspberries, strawberries and pomegranate seeds are such perfect size shapes that there is no point in doing anything more than rinsing off the dirt.

One of the chief pleasures of fruit salad is its juice. To achieve the best results squeeze the juice from citrus fruits such as oranges or limes, and pour over the fruit, leaving it to stand for a few hours while flavours of the fruits and juice mingle.

Here are suggestions for fruit to use in a winter fruit salad.

1 medium banana
1 pear, diced
1 apple, diced
4 clementines
175 g (6 oz) lychees
6 fresh dates, chopped fine
juice of 1 large orange
brandy (optional)

Peel and slice the banana and put in a bowl together with the diced apple and pear. Peel the clementines and break into segments, removing any pith. Peel the lychees and cut the flesh away from the pip. Chop the dates into quarters and mix well with all the other fruit. Squeeze the juice from the orange and pour over the fruit. If it is a festive occasion add a teaspoon or two of brandy.

Makes 6 portions. Each one is 25 g CHO. 95 kcals.

Dried Fruit Compote

The dried fruit makes an intensely sweet liquid which can be considerably diluted and still taste sweet. Dried peaches, with their fabulous rich flavour, are an unusual addition to this dessert. Although only a small amount is used, the peaches swell up while soaking. About 2.5 kg (5lbs) of fresh peaches go into making 450 g (1lb) of dried ones.

75 g (3 oz) pitted prunes
25 g (1 oz) dried peaches
50 g (2 oz) dried apple rings
50 g (2 oz) dried apricots
800 ml (1 pt 7 fl oz) spring water

7.5 cm (3 inches) lemon rind
7.5 cm (3 inches) orange rind
1 cinnamon stick
150 g (5 oz) green grapes, with pips removed

Rinse the dried fruit and leave to soak for at least an hour in the spring water. Pour the fruit and liquid in a large saucepan and add the lemon and orange rind and cinnamon stick. Bring to the boil and simmer for 30 minutes, until the fruit is softened. Remove from the heat and add the grapes. The soft green colour adds contrast to the muted hues and textures of the dried fruit. Cool. Remove the orange and lemon rind and cinnamon stick and serve with ladles full of juice.

Makes 6 servings. Each serving is 20 g CHO. 80 kcals.

Pear Compote with Orange

My sister-in-law, who has a very sweet tooth, recommends this superb way of cooking pears. William pears work well in this recipe.

500 g (1 lb 2 oz) firm pears
1–2 cloves

2 large oranges weighing about 500 g (1 lb 2 oz)

Wash the pears and slice them, then put into a heavy based saucepan. Squeeze the juice from one of the oranges and pour over the fruit. Peel the other orange, making sure to remove the pith, and cut it into thin slices. Add them and the cloves to the pears. Bring to the boil and simmer, covered, on a very low heat so that the water is barely bubbling for about 10–15 minutes, until softened.

Makes 4 portions. Each portion is 17.5 g CHO. 70 kcals.

Apricot Compote

Visits to the greengrocer in the 1990s offer a wide variety of fruit and even a choice of country of origin. The morning I tested this recipe the greengrocer offered me Spanish or Greek apricots. The Spanish ones were large and a light yellow. The Greek ones had a deeper coloured skin and were small. I had seen them in the shops before and thought I would experiment to see if their flavour was more concentrated. They worked very well in this recipe.

600 g (1 lb 5 oz) apricots
100 g (4 oz) ripe pear,
  peeled
100 ml (4 fl oz) unsweet-
  ened apple juice

100 ml (4 fl oz) water
½ tsp finely grated orange
  zest (use an organic
  orange)

Wash the apricots and cut in half with a sharp knife, removing the stone. Set the apricot halves aside on a plate.
  Use a pear that is beginning to soften. Cut it into small pieces and place it in a pan with the juice and water. Bring to the boil and add the finely grated orange zest. Allow this mixture to simmer for a few minutes and then mash the pear with the back of a fork so that it flakes into the liquid.
  Place the apricots, skin side down, in the pan and simmer, covered, for 5–10 minutes, until they begin to soften. If you leave them for longer they will disintegrate.

Transfer from the pan to an attractive serving bowl and leave to cool. Serve at room temperature or chill in the fridge depending on preference. The recipe makes a lot of juice.

Makes 4 servings. Each serving is 15 g CHO. 60 kcals

Pineapple Filled with Exotic Fruit

This recipe always reminds me of the 'Brazilian Bombshell' Carmen Miranda, who went on stage to sing sambas with exotic fruit on her head. Serve this dish to the background of *The Lady with the Tutti Frutti Hat!*

1 large pineapple
2 kiwis weighing about
   125 g (4½ oz)
2 large ripe figs weighing
   about 150 g (5 oz)

125 g (4½ oz) fresh dates
1 carambola or starfruit
Juice from 1 lime

Cut a 2.5–3.5 cm (1–1½ inch) deep lid from the top of the pineapple. You can either leave the plume intact or trim. Put it aside for decoration.

Remove the flesh from the pineapple by cutting about 1.2 cm (½ inch) away from the skin all the way round. Avoid puncturing the skin because it serves as a container for the fruit. Remove the core and dice the flesh into small chunks and place in a bowl. It should make about 400 g (14 oz).

Peel the kiwis and chop into small pieces. Quarter the figs and slice thinly. Squeeze off the skin from the dates and chop the flesh. Slice the carambola to make its typical star shape. Mix all the fruit with the pineapple. Add the lime juice and leave to chill in the fridge for a couple of hours. Pile as much of the fruit as possible into the pineapple shell and top with the pineapple lid. Serve immediately.

Makes 4 large portions. Each portion is 25 g CHO. 100 kcals.

Papaya the Pleasant

Papayas look unexciting in their greenish coloured skins but peel them and you will find a luscious pink fruit, with large black seeds. Marco Polo credited papaya with saving his ship's crew from scurvy. Certainly, it contains as much vitamin C as lime and a good deal of carotene. Two elderly Turkish sisters, who used to make a great fuss of my young daughter, suggested on hearing that she had diabetes that she ate papaya to improve her constititution. They were quite rare at the time but I managed to find one. She did not like the taste. I was never sure how it was meant to help.

1 large papaya weighing about 400 g (14 oz)
1 small galia melon weighing 700 g (1 lb 9 oz) without seeds

1 orange weighing about 150 g (5 oz) (use an organic orange)

Peel the papaya and cut it into small chunks. Using a special cutter, cut the melon into balls. Peel the orange skin thinly, pour boiling water over it, and leave for one minute. Slice into small strips and mix with the fruit. Squeeze the juice from the orange and pour over the fruit. Leave to chill for at least 3 hours before serving.

Makes 4 portions. Each portion is 15 g CHO. 70 kcals.

Red Fruit Dessert

All these fruits are found in the shops during July. The fruit dish is garnished with frozen redcurrants. Their frosty look and hard texture makes an interesting contrast with the other fruits.

Use well-ripened redcurrants otherwise they tend to be sour. Like raspberries they contain some iron, magnesium and calcium.

150 g (5 oz) redcurrants	200 g (7 oz) raspberries
200 g (7 oz) strawberries	2 tbs unsweetened apple
200 g (7 oz) cherries	juice

Wash and dry the redcurrants. Take 50 g (2 oz) of them and lay them flat in a plastic container and freeze until frozen hard – about three hours.

Wash and hull the strawberries and cut into slices. Wash and slice the cherries. Take 4 serving glasses and divide the strawberries equally between them. Place the cherries on top of the strawberries. The third layer is the redcurrants and they are topped with the washed raspberries. Pour a dessertspoon of apple juice over each portion and leave to chill in the fridge for 3 hours. When ready to serve, garnish each glass with some of the frozen redcurrants.

Makes 4 servings. Each serving is 15 g CHO. 60 kcals

Melon Cups

Walking into my local health food shop one morning I found an array of small yellow organic honeydew melons. They were expensive but Carl, the owner and former Jungian psychotherapist, had me reaching for my purse when he assured me they were so good that they were selling like hot cakes in France. This dessert works as well with large honeydew melons but the small ones provide perfect individual-sized portions.

2 small honeydew melons, each weighing 600 g (1 lb 5 oz) without the seeds	450 g (1 lb) strawberries 2 kiwis ½ lime

Cut the melons in half and remove the seeds. Use a special cutter to make balls from the melon flesh. Put them in a bowl.

Wash, dry and hull the strawberries. If they are small, leave them as they are; but if large, cut into quarters and mix with the melon balls. Peel the kiwis and cut them into thin slices. Peel the lime, chop finely and add to the other fruit. Chill in the fridge for 3 hours. Spoon into the four hollow halves of the melon and serve. If you want to increase the firmness of the melon shells put them in the freezer for one hour before they are needed.

Makes 4 portions. Each portion is 20 g CHO. 90 kcals.

Mango-Cherry Cool

Mangoes and cherries are both very sweet fruits with striking colours. Serve them together and you have a refreshing dessert that satisfies the visual senses as well as the taste buds.

Mangoes are ready to eat when the skin gives a little to pressure from the finger. If they are rock-hard leave them to ripen in a brown paper bag for a couple of days.

400 g (14 oz) peeled mango 250 g (9 oz) cherries 1 tbs unsweetened apple juice	juice of 1 lime 450 g (1 lb) low-fat fromage frais

Dice the mango and put it in a bowl. Cut the cherries in half and remove the stones. Combine the two fruits and mix them with the apple juice and the freshly squeezed lime juice. Leave to stand in the fridge for a few hours.

Assemble by putting 75 g (3 oz) of fromage frais in the bottom of each serving glass and spoon the fruit and a little juice on top.

Makes 6 servings. Each serving is 20 g CHO. 100 kcals

White and Red Fruit

Tayberries are a cross between blackberries and raspberries. The sculpted form looks like an elongated blackberry and is a soft maroon colour.

350 g (12 oz) white nectarines
350 g (12 oz) peaches
100 g (4 oz) raspberries
150 g (5 oz) tayberries

3 tbs unsweetened apple juice
2 tbs freshly squeezed lime juice

Melba Sauce recipe (page 150)

Wash the nectarines and peaches and dry them. Thinly slice the nectarines keeping the skin on. Peel the peaches and slice thinly into strips. Mix them together in a bowl and add the rinsed raspberries and tayberries. Mix the apple and lime juice and pour over the fruit. Mix gently with a large spoon. Leave to chill in the fridge for at least a couple of hours before serving.

Prepare the Melba Sauce and pour over the fruit bowl just before serving.

Makes 6 servings. Each serving with sauce is 25 g CHO. 100 kcals.

Summer Pudding

This is a classic summer dessert – a colourful mixture of soft berries packed in a bread mould dyed scarlet by the juices of the fruits.

Redcurrants strengthen the colour of the juice but beware sour ones. The sweetest redcurrants are picked at the end of their short season. Don't skimp with the quality of bread. An unexciting wholemeal loaf will only be partially disguised by the fruit juice – a fresh farmhouse loaf will provide much more flavour.

10 slices of wholemeal bread with crusts removed weighing about 200 g (7 oz)
275 g (10 oz) strawberries

275 g (10 oz) raspberries
150 g (5 oz) redcurrants
2 tsp arrowroot
150 ml (5 fl oz) unsweetened apple juice

Use a pudding basin or deep glass bowl. Cut out a base for the bowl from a slice of bread. Put 1 or 2 slices aside for the lid. Cut each of the remaining ones into three fingers and place these around the side. Tuck them behind the bread base and let the sides slightly overlap. Gently press the sides down against each other.

In a stainless steel saucepan, mix the arrowroot with the apple juice. Pour in the rinsed soft fruit and slowly bring to the boil and simmer for about 2 minutes, until the fruit is soft and some liquid has been released into the apple juice.

Spoon the fruit and some of the liquid into the bread-lined bowl. Cover the top with the remaining pieces of bread. Pour the rest of the liquid over the bread cover. Cover the top of the basin or bowl with a plate and put it in the fridge with a weight on top to press it down – a full jar of jam is about right as a weight. Leave overnight. Just before serving the pudding, turn it out of the dish by loosening the sides with a knife and then inverting it on to a plate.

Makes 6 large servings. Each serving is 25 g CHO. 115 kcals

Crepes, Pancakes and Fritters

Do recipes like these have a place in a low-fat diet? Yes, provided you use an oil such as sunflower which is high in polyunsaturates and if you fry correctly. What this means for pancakes and crepes is to use a seasoned, heavy-based, frying pan – one that is not scoured each time after use but cleaned with salt and kitchen paper so that it needs very little oil poured over the surface to stop the pancake sticking.

Fritters are fried in deeper oil. If the base of the pan is not too wide – 15 cm (6 inches) is adequate – and the oil is hot, the fritters brown quickly and soak up very little oil. Always place on kitchen paper to absorb any surplus oil. Incorrect frying makes food greasy but the results will always be good if you use a utensil you are confident with, can easily increase or decrease the cooking temperature, and serve immediately.

Blintz

Traditionally blintzes are thin pancakes filled with a white cheese mixture, often slightly sweetened and served with sour cream. Everybody has their own variation on this theme – in America they are sometimes stuffed with blueberries, in Britain the trend is to serve them fairly sweet. This recipe is a sugar-free version.

Batter
100 g (4 oz) wholewheat
  flour
2 eggs
2 tsp oil (optional)
225 ml (8 fl oz) skimmed
  milk

Filling
225 g (8 oz) low-fat curd
  cheese
100 g (4 oz) cottage cheese
1 egg yolk
75 g (3 oz) raisins
few drops of vanilla
  essence

For the batter, put the flour in a large bowl and make a well in the centre. Lightly beat the eggs and oil and pour into the well. Gradually add flour to the egg and oil mixture until all the flour has been absorbed. Add the milk. (Some wholewheat flours need more liquid than others). If the final batter mix seems thick, add an extra 25 ml (1 fl oz) milk.) For a very light and airy batter whizz the ingredients together in a blender. Leave to stand in the fridge for at least 30 minutes.

Prepare the filling: wash the raisins and pat dry. Put the cottage cheese through a food mill so that all the lumps are removed and mix with the curd cheese. Lightly whisk the egg yolk with a fork and add. Stir in the raisins and vanilla essence.

Fry the pancakes in whatever size frying pan you find comfortable to use. Ideally it should be a well-seasoned pan that is kept for omelettes and is not scoured clean between each use. If it tends to stick, improve it by rubbing the inside surface with oil, heat the frying pan until it is hot and then wipe the oil off.

Heat the pan and when it is hot spread a small amount of oil over the surface. Pour in a few tablespoons of the batter and tilt the pan quickly so that it spreads thinly over the entire pan. If there is any excess batter return it to the bowl. When the top side is set, remove from the pan and transfer to a plate. Cover the pancake with greaseproof paper to prevent it drying up. Repeat this procedure until the batter is used up. The number of pancakes depends on the size of the frying pan.

Fill the pancake by placing it brown side up and putting a heaped tablespoon of the filling along the centre. Roll the pancake over the filling once, fold the sides over towards the centre and finish rolling. Lightly butter a baking dish and lay the blintzes in it. Bake in a moderate oven, gas 4/ 350°F/180°C for 15 minutes until the blintzes are warmed through. The outside of the blintz should still be soft. An alternative method is to fry them on both sides in a mixture of butter and oil.

Eat them as they are or serve with fromage frais or Cinnamon Ice Cream (page 100)

Makes 8 blintz. Each blintz is 15 g CHO. 180 kcals

Strawberry Crepes

The secret of successful crepes is to make them very thin by spreading a small amount of batter over the surface of the pan before it can set. Tilting the pan is an effective method. A French cookbook from the late Middle Ages, *Menagier de Paris*, recommends using 'a bowl pierced with a hole as large as your little finger; then put some of the batter in the bowl and, beginning in the middle, let it pour all around the pan.'

1 recipe Blintz Batter (page 52)

Strawberry topping
450 g (1 lb) strawberries

100 ml (4 fl oz) white Chardonnay wine
100 ml (4 fl oz) unsweetened apple juice

To make the pancakes drop a spoonful of oil (the size of the spoon depends on the size of the pan) into the frying pan and swirl it over the base so that it is thinly coated. When the oil is hot pour in just enough batter to cover the base. As the underside of the pancake browns turn it over to brown the other side. Continue with the remainder of the batter.

The pancakes can be prepared in advance and stored with sheets of greaseproof paper between them in the fridge.

Wash and hull the strawberries and place them in a medium-sized pan with the wine and juice. Bring to the boil and simmer for two minutes so that the juice turns pink. Remove the strawberries with a slotted spoon and wrap them in the crepes. Let the remaining liquid boil for a further minute or two to thicken. Pour it over the crepes and serve. It is not a good idea to prepare the strawberries in advance because their fresh taste will wane.

Makes 6 crepes. Each one is 20 g CHO. 200 kcals.

Fried Cherries

This may sound sinful but a cherry dipped in batter and quickly fried in hot oil becomes even juicier and more desirable than usual. Try serving with scoops of Banana Ice Cream (page 91).

325 g (11 oz) black cherries

Batter
50 g (2 oz) wholewheat
   flour

¼ tsp ground cinnamon
   (optional)
90–100 ml (3½–4 fl oz) water
1 small egg white
oil for frying

Wash and stone the cherries.

Gradually combine the flour and cinammon with the water to make a thick paste. Leave to stand in the fridge for one hour. The texture will be much more elastic when you remove it from the fridge. Whisk the egg white into stiff peaks and stir into the paste to make a very thick batter.

Pour oil to a depth of about 2.5 cm (1 inch) into a small pan, so that the cherries can be fried a few at a time but very fast. If you like your batter coating thin, thread about 4 cherries on to a chopstick and dip into the batter. Drop the cherries off into the hot oil. If you prefer a thicker coating that gives more to sink your teeth into, then roll them in the batter with your fingers until well coated and then drop into the hot oil. The coated cherries cook quickly. Turn them over so that they brown evenly.

All the fried cherries are 70 g CHO. 450 kcals.

Yogurt Pancakes with Apple Sauce

These pancakes are very light and quick to make. Although they are made with yogurt they do not have a marked yogurt taste, particularly if you use one of the live yogurts which have a milder taste than low-fat natural yogurt. Reluctant yogurt-eaters will tuck into this beneficial food without complaints.

Batter
100 g (4 oz) wholewheat
   flour
½ tsp bicarbonate of soda
2 eggs
250 ml (9 fl oz) low-fat
   natural yogurt or live
   yogurt

2 tbs oil

Apple Sauce
450 g (1 lb) eating apples
200 ml (7 fl oz) water

For the sauce, slice the apples thinly and bring to the boil with the water. Continue boiling over a medium heat until virtually all the water is absorbed and the apples are soft. Blend into a thick sauce and cover until needed.

Pour the flour and bicarbonate of soda into a bowl and crack the eggs into a well in the centre. Lightly beat the eggs with a fork and gradually work in a little of the flour at a time. This avoids lumps forming. When all the flour is worked into a thick paste, gradually stir in the yogurt and the oil. The batter is now ready for cooking. If you intend to store it in the fridge for an hour or so add the bicarbonate of soda just before cooking.

Cover the base of a frying pan with a thin layer of oil. Heat and drop tablespoons of the batter into the pan. The oil should start sizzling immediately. Lower the heat a little so that the small pancakes continue cooking fairly vigorously but do not brown too quickly. As holes begin to appear on the upper surface turn them over. When lightly browned, remove and serve with a spoonful of the apple sauce.

Makes 20 small pancakes. Each pancake is 4 g CHO. 60 kcals. Each pancake served with apple sauce is 5 g CHO. 70 kcals.

Indonesian Banana Fritters

Coconut milk is used in South Indian and South-east Asian cookery. It can be found in any grocers that specialize in food from those regions. Shake the tin well before using as the water and coconut often separate. It should be very thick. If you want to make it yourself, pour 450 ml (¾ pt) of boiling water over 225 g (8 oz) desiccated coconut. Blend in the processor until well mixed. Leave to cool to hand-temperature. Lift out handfuls of the coconut and squeeze over a sieve to extract the maximum amount of coconut milk. This should make 250–300 ml (9–11 fl oz) of coconut milk.

The fritters eaten straight from the frying pan are puffy and crisp – if you keep them warm in an oven before serving they are still delicious but lose their crispness.

50 g (2 oz) brown rice flour
50 g (2 oz) wholewheat
   flour
1 egg, slightly beaten
150–175 ml (5–6 fl oz) coconut milk
4 large, peeled bananas
   weighing about 160 g (5½
   oz) each

Orange Sauce
200 ml (7 fl oz) unsweet-
   ened orange juice or the
   juice of 2 medium
   oranges
1½–2 tsp arrowroot

Combine the two flours. Make a well in the centre and add the beaten egg. Gradually beat a little of the flour into the egg to form a smooth paste. Gradually add the coconut milk, beating in more of the flour until a thick coating batter is formed. Leave to stand for 15 minutes.

Prepare the sauce: combine the arrowroot with a little of the liquid to make a smooth paste. Add the rest of the liquid and heat over a low light until it comes to the boil and thickens. Allow to simmer for a few minutes, stirring all the time.

Frying the fritters: cut the bananas in half and then lengthways to make 4 pieces from each. Dip them in the batter so that they are well-coated and fry in hot oil about 2.5 cm (1 inch) deep.

Test the heat of the oil by dropping in a breadcrumb – if it drops to the bottom and then rises to the surface, the oil is the right temperature. If it stays on the surface immediately it is too hot. The heat is more concentrated in a small container and the cooking process is quicker so that the food soaks up less oil. Fry for a couple of minutes until both sides are crisp and brown. Drain on absorbent paper. Serve hot with a little of the warm sauce.

Makes 16. Each fritter and sauce is 10 g CHO. 80 kcals.

Jellies, Creams and Mousses

Manufactured mousses and jellies brought joy to supermarket balance sheets in the 1980s. All, so far as I can tell, sweetened unhealthily. When making your own, all you need is fruit purée and yogurt or fromage frais, a setting agent and the occasional egg. Exploit your supermarket only for exotic fruits.

I normally make jelly with agar-agar powder – the vegetarian seaweed setting agent – but at the time of preparing this book the health food shops only stocked the flakes. They are as effective as the powder but have to be heated longer and more slowly.

If the powder becomes available again use half the amount specified for the flakes. Mix with a little water before adding to the rest of the liquid and boil for 1½ minutes.

Fruit Jelly Ring

300 g (11 oz) strawberries
1 kiwi
75 g (3 oz) small seedless
  grapes
1 passion fruit

400 ml (14 fl oz) unsweetened apple juice
100 ml (4 fl oz) water
2 tbs agar-agar flakes

Wash, hull and pat dry the strawberries. Slice thinly. Peel the kiwi and slice it thinly. Wash and dry the grapes.

Dissolve the agar-agar flakes in the water and about 100 ml (4 fl oz) of the apple juice. Bring to the boil and then allow to simmer, stirring with a wooden spoon, for 5 minutes. Add the remaining apple juice and quickly bring to the boil. Remove immediately from the heat.

Place half the slices of strawberries and kiwi around the base and sides of a ring mould. Pour over enough jelly to cover them. Leave to almost set then arrange the remaining strawberries and the grapes on top. Scoop out the passion fruit and mix with the remaining apple jelly and pour over the fruit so that it is completely covered. The reason for pouring the jelly in two stages is to allow the jelly to set in the spaces between the fruit, separating them.

Chill the jelly in the fridge. When ready to serve, insert a knife around the outer and inner edges of the mould. Immerse the mould for 5 seconds in a bowl of warm water and dry the outside. Place a plate over the top and invert the mould. Gently lift the mould off the jelly on to the plate. It can be served with fresh fruit piled in the middle.

Makes 8 small servings. Each serving is 12.5 g CHO. 50 kcals.

Nectarine Jelly Cups

When blending the nectarines for this jelly don't bother to peel the fruit. Its red skin gives a pleasant speckled effect.

4 nectarines weighing about 500 g (1 lb 2 oz)
100 ml (4 fl oz) unsweetened apple juice
50 g (2 oz) peeled banana (optional, use if nectarines are not especially ripe)
75 ml (3 fl oz) water
100 ml (4 fl oz) unsweetened orange juice
2 tbs agar-agar flakes

Wash and dry the nectarines. Slice them into a liquidizer and blend with the apple juice and banana to make a thick fruit purée.

Dissolve the agar-agar flakes in the water in a small pan. Add the orange juice. Bring to the boil and then simmer for five minutes, stirring all the time with a wooden spoon until the liquid is reduced to about 100 ml (4 fl oz). Add to the nectarine purée and stir in well. Spoon into four elegant glass bowls and leave to set.

Makes 4 cups of jelly. Each cup is 20 g CHO. 85 kcals.

Apple Snow

This is a light and easy dish to make. If you want it to have more substance serve with Cinnamon Sticks (page 147).

4 large eating apples
  weighing about 550 g (1
  lb 4 oz)
150 ml (5 fl oz) unsweet-
  ened apple juice

1 large egg white
flaked almonds
ground cinnamon

Wash and slice the apples and put them in a saucepan with the apple juice. Bring to the boil and then simmer on a low heat with the pan covered until the fruit is softened and much of the juice is absorbed. Remove from the heat and allow to cool.

Pour the fruit and liquid into a blender and whizz into a fruit purée, or use a food mill or sieve. Whisk the egg white until it forms stiff peaks and stir gently into the apple. Pour into four individual serving bowls and decorate the top with a few almonds. Sprinkle these with a little cinnamon.

Makes 4 servings. Each serving is 17.5 g CHO. 75 kcals.

Peach Parfait

When casting an eye over rows of peaches on the green-grocer's shelf it is not always obvious which are ripe and ready to eat. The ideal is juicy and sweet, the reality is often hard and sour or soft and tasteless. Peaches can be left to ripen at home but they tend to soften and wither as well. The essence of the problem is that peaches are picked to survive transportation and distribution to the shops – very different considerations from the ones you make when picking them in the garden. Despite all this some good quality peaches are getting through. Look out for Italian cling stones and for vine peaches at your greengrocer's or Marks and Spencers or Sainsburys.

Peaches, like all the yellowy-orange coloured fruits, are high in carotene and also contain substantial amounts of potassium.

4 peaches weighing about
   650 g (1 lb 7 oz)
3 tbs unsweetened apple
   juice
pinch ground ginger

½-1 tbs cognac (optional)
2 tbs arrowroot
about 100 ml (4 fl oz) low
   fat natural or live
   yogurt

Pour boiling water over two of the peaches and leave for about 2 minutes. Remove them from the water and peel. Cut into thin slices and put to one side.

Blend the remaining two peaches with the apple juice. Pour the fruit purée into a medium sized stainless steel saucepan with the ginger and brandy. Take off a dessert-spoon of the liquid, mix with the arrowroot and pour it back into the pan. Bring to the boil and simmer for 2 minutes, stirring with a wooden spoon as the fruit purée thickens. Add the slices of peach and bring to the boil for about 15 seconds and then transfer to a bowl to cool.

Lay out 4 serving glasses or dishes and divide almost all of the fruit mixture between them. Put a tablespoon of yogurt on top of the fruit then cover with half a tablespoon of the purée. Finally top with a teaspoon of yogurt.

Makes 4 servings. Each serving is 17.5 g CHO. 80 kcals.

Plum Fool

A classic fruit fool is not only puréed fruit and cream mixed together but includes custard as well. The custard can be made with or without arrowroot. The arrowroot reduces the amount of time you spend standing over the cooker stirring away. Using arrowroot, it takes only a couple of minutes, without the arrowroot it involves about 10 minutes of stirring. Half a teaspoon of arrowroot is only about 10 calories.

275 g (10 oz) yellow plums
50 ml (2 fl oz) unsweetened
   apple juice

Custard
1 large egg yolk

1 tsp arrowroot (optional)
150 ml (5 fl oz) skimmed
   milk
125 g (4½ oz) peeled banana
75 g (3 oz) Greek yogurt

Wash and dry the plums and slice them into a blender. Pour in the apple juice and whizz for a few seconds into a fruit purée.

Lightly beat the egg yolk with a fork and then add the arrowroot, if using.

Heat the milk in a small saucepan to just below boiling point. Pour the milk over the yolk, stirring. Pour the egg and milk mixture back into the pan on a very low heat. Stir continuously with a wooden spoon until the mixture thickens and coats the back of the spoon. If the contents of the pan seem to be getting too hot remove the pan from the heat or it holding a little way above the heat. The custard should not be allowed to boil as this causes curdling.

When the custard has thickened, prepare the banana by sieving it or putting it through a food mill, then add it to the custard. Stir in the fruit purée and yogurt. Chill before serving.

Makes 4 servings. Each serving is 15 g CHO. 110 kcals.

Peach Whip

This cream has a spicey taste. It can be served by itself or in tall glasses with a dollop of fromage frais on top. If fresh peaches are unavailable use tinned peaches in apple juice.

Arrowroot, like potato flour, is a root starch used for thickening. The advantage of using arrowroot rather than cornflour, which is made from grains, is that it is tasteless so does not need to be precooked for a long time to get rid of its raw taste. An additional advantage is that smaller amounts can be used to achieve the same thickening results. It thickens more quickly because it forms an emulsion at lower temperatures than flour or cornflour.

50 g (2 oz) dried dates
100 ml (4 fl oz) water
550 g (1 lb 4 oz) ripe
   peaches
100 ml (4 fl oz) unsweet-
   ened apple juice
50 g (2 oz) peeled ripe
   banana

2 tsp arrowroot
100 ml (4 fl oz) Greek
   yogurt
pinch freshly grated nut-
   meg

Heat the dried dates and water in a small pan until the

water is almost absorbed and the dates can be mashed with a fork.

Slice the peaches with their skins on into the blender with the apple juice, mashed dates and banana and whizz for a few seconds to make a smooth fruit purée. Pour the purée into a pan, add the arrowroot mixed with a tablespoon of water and simmer for a minute or two until it has thickened.

Remove the fruit from the heat and leave to cool. Stir in the yogurt and nutmeg. Chill for two hours before serving.

Makes 4 large servings. Each serving is 25 g CHO. 135 kcals.

Carob-Kumquat Cheese Bombes

Kumquats originate in China and their Cantonese name *Kam Kwat* means 'gold orange'. They are tiny compared to oranges and bullet-shaped rather than round, but they contain over 50 per cent more carotene. They are also a source of calcium, magnesium and potassium.

This soft cheese dessert requires no baking but is left to firm in the fridge. It has a firm, velvety texture and is a very light brown colour. The carob flavour is background rather than dominant.

The mixture is poured into individual moulds and removed just before serving. To facilitate removal the containers can be lined with muslin or, if none is available, use gauze bandages opened up to the thinnest layer and cut to shape.

For the carob flavour use a good quality carob bar. If buying an unfamiliar brand always check the ingredients listed on the wrapping to make sure no sugar is included. I find that the bars made in Cyprus and found in health food shops are suitable for this recipe.

100 g (4 oz) kumquats
100 ml (4 fl oz) freshly
    squeezed or unsweet-
    ened orange juice
75 g (3 oz) dried dates,
    finely sliced
25 g (1 oz) peeled ripe
    banana, mashed

50 g (2 oz) carob bar,
    unsweetened
225 g (8 oz) low-fat curd
    cheese
50 g (2 oz) low-fat yogurt

Wash the kumquats. They are not used peeled. Slice the
ends off. Squeeze the juice into a small saucepan. Slice and
chop the remaining kumquat. Discard the pips and any
thick pithy pieces and add the chopped kumquat to the
saucepan. Add the orange juice, dates and mashed banana.
(If using a food processor these ingredients can be chopped
finely before putting in the saucepan.)

Carefully bring to the boil and then reduce to a low heat,
stirring all the time with a wooden spoon. Continue to cook
the ingredients in this way for about five minutes, until the
kumquats soften and form a thick paste-like texture.
Remove from the heat.

Break the carob bar into pieces and put in a bowl over a
shallow pan of boiling water until it melts. (If using a micro-
wave remember that carob takes longer than chocolate to
melt.)

Mix the curd cheese and yogurt together. Fold in the fruit
mixture well. Add a dessertspoon at a time of this mixture
to the melted carob until half has been added. Then add the
remainder at one go.

Fill ramekins or any other attractive containersthat you
possess with the cheese mixture. I use some pretty Japanese tea cups which when inverted give a rounded shape.
If serving this dessert in the containers there is no need to
line them. If inverting them line with muslin or gauze.

Smooth the tops with a knife. Leave to stand in the fridge for at least four hours to set firm.

Makes 5 portions. Each one is 20 g CHO. 160 kcals.

Mango Curd Cheeses

Individual white cheese portions with a layer of mango underneath make a light, balmy dessert. As in all recipes that use mango, success depends on the sweetness of the fruit. I used Indian mangoes, which are said to be the sweetest of all. When they are ripe they are an even musty yellow colour – avoid any that have dark marks on the skin.

Mango filling
350 g (12 oz) ripe mango flesh
3 tbs unsweetened apple juice
1 egg yolk

Cheesecake
25 g (1 oz) dried dates
50 ml (2 fl oz) water
225 g (8 oz) low fat curd cheese
100 g (4 oz) fromage frais
100 g (4 oz) peeled ripe banana
1 egg + 1 egg white

Heat the oven (gas 4/350°F/180°C).

Blend the mango, apple juice and egg yolk in a liquidizer or processor. If using a hand-operated food mill, sieve the fruit and whisk in the egg yolk and apple juice. Divide the fruit mixture between 6 ramekins.

Heat the dates and the water in a small pan on a low heat until all the water has been absorbed by the dates and a thick paste has formed. Mash with a fork to break up any large pieces. Leave until cool.

Combine the curd cheese and fromage frais. Sieve the

banana or put it through a food mill to form a smooth liquid. Add this purée to the cheeses. Add the cooled date paste. Whisk the eggs and stir in.

Gently spoon the cheese mixture over the mango. The cheese mixture is heavier than the mango and if it is poured too quickly over the fruit base, the mango will tend to rise up at the sides. Bake for 15–20 minutes until the top of the cheese has set but has not yet turned brown at the edge.

Chill in the fridge before serving.

Makes 6 portions. Each one is 17.5 g CHO. 125 kcals.

Poppy Seed Mousse

50 g (2 oz) poppy seed
250 g (9 oz) eating apples
200 ml (7 fl oz) water
40 g (1½ oz) sultanas
50 ml (2 fl oz) unsweetened
  apple juice

1 tbs agar-agar flakes
75 g (3 oz) low-fat fromage
  frais
1 egg white, stiffly whisked

Grind the poppy seeds well in an electric coffee grinder or the small cup of a food processor.

Slice the apple into a medium-sized pan with the water, apple juice and sultanas and simmer until the apples are beginning to soften. Blend. Return to the pan and add the agar-agar flakes, stirring for five minutes as it cooks over a low heat. Remove from the heat and add the ground poppy seed. Leave to cool for a few minutes. Whisk the egg white until stiff. Fold the fromage frais and egg white into the apple mixture. Pour into an attractive bowl ready for serving. Chill in the fridge once the mixture has cooled.

Makes 6 portions. Each portion is 12.5 g CHO. 95 kcals.

Gooseberry Mousse

400 g (14 oz) ripe gooseberries
1½ tbs agar-agar flakes
400 ml (14 fl oz) unsweetened apple juice

100 g (4 oz) firm tofu
1 egg white
few raw pistachio nuts,
  finely chopped

Dissolve the agar-agar in 2 tablespoons of water.

Wash and top and tail the gooseberries. Put them in a heavy-based saucepan with the apple juice and simmer on a low heat until they are soft. Stir in the agar-agar flakes and keep on stirring for five minutes over a low heat. Blend with the tofu to make a thick, creamy mixture. Leave to cool. Whisk the egg white stiffly and fold into the cooled mixture. Pour into 4 tall glasses and chill in the fridge. Garnish with the pistachio nuts.

Makes 4 servings. Each serving is 25 g CHO. 110 kcals.

Carob Mousse

This is a mousse made without any egg. It can be served by itself, garnished with fruit or nuts or served with Almond Thins (page 148).

150 g (5 oz) ricotta cheese
75 g (3 oz) carob bar,
  broken in pieces
150 ml (5 fl oz) low-fat
  yogurt
1 tsp brandy (optional)

1 heaped dessertspoon
  agar-agar flakes
3 tbs freshly squeezed or
  unsweetened orange
  juice
3 tbs water

Mash the ricotta cheese finely with a fork.

Place the broken pieces of carob in a bowl in a pan of

shallow boiling water. Add the yogurt and as the carob begins to melt stir together to make a dark brown cream. Remove from the heat and pour in the ricotta cheese and mix well. Add the brandy, if using.

Place the agar-agar flakes in a pan with the orange juice and water and simmer for 5 minutes, stirring all the time with a wooden spoon. Pour into the carob cream and spoon into 4 small serving bowls. Chill in the fridge before serving.

Makes 4 portions. Each portion is 15 g CHO. 190 kcals.

Sultana Cream

Serve with cakes, fresh fruit or by itself.

50 g (2 oz) sultanas   200 g (7 oz) fromage frais

Wash the sultanas and put them in a small saucepan with 100 ml (4 fl oz) water. Simmer until the water is absorbed and blend the sultanas in an electric grinder to a paste. Mix well with the fromage frais and store covered in the fridge for use the same day.

The cream is 40 g CHO. 215 kcals.

Cinnamon-Banana Cream

This is a quick, uncooked sauce to spoon over fruit and puddings or eat by itself.

150 g (5 oz) peeled ripe   150 g (5 oz) low-fat
  banana   fromage frais
                                              ¼ tsp ground cinnamon

Sieve the banana or put through a food mill so that it becomes liquid. Mix in with the fromage frais and cinnamon. Chill before using.

Cream is 35 g CHO. 185 kcals.

Triflettes

These mini-trifles are made with a light fruit sauce instead of custard.

Apricot Sauce
450 g (1 lb) apricots
1 eating apple weighing
   about 125 g (4½ oz),
   sliced
75 ml (3 fl oz) water
pinch mixed spice
2 tsp ground arrowroot

¼ tsp ground cardamom
few drops of vanilla
   essence
1 tbs Grand Marnier
   (optional)
2 tbs freshly squeezed or
   unsweetened orange
   juice

Spiced Sponge
2 eggs
90 g (3½ oz) peeled banana
40 g (1½ oz generous)
   wholewheat flour
½ tsp cinnamon
½ tsp mixed spice

Topping
600 g (1 lb 5 oz) low-fat
   fromage frais
300 g (11 oz) seedless green
   and black grapes (use
   only green if black are
   not available), halved

Prepare the apricot sauce: wash and halve the apricots and remove the stones. Place the apricots in a medium saucepan with the sliced apple and water. Neither of the fruits need be peeled. Bring to the boil and simmer for a few minutes until lightly softened. Pour the fruit and liquid into the blender with the spice and whizz for a few seconds to form a fruit purée.

Return this mixture to the saucepan. Take off a dessert-spoon of the liquid to mix with the arrowroot, then pour back into the mixture. Bring to the boil and simmer for one minute. A stainless steel pan reduces the chance of the fruit sauce catching and burning. Pour the thickened sauce into a bowl to cool.

Prepare the sponge: separate the yolks and the whites of the eggs. Whisk the egg yolks until they are creamy. Mash the banana with a fork and whisk with the egg yolks until a smooth texture is achieved. Fold in the flour, spices and vanilla essence. Whisk the egg whites until they are standing in stiff peaks and fold into the mixture. Cover the base of a 25 × 20 cm (10 × 8 inch) baking tin with greased parchment paper. Bake in a preheated oven (gas 6/400°F/ 200°C) for 7–10 minutes until lightly browned. Remove from the tin onto a wire tray to cool. Drizzle the combined Grand Marnier and orange juice over the surface. Leave to soak in.

Assemble the triflettes: spoon the fruit sauce between six glasses or serving bowls. Cut the soaked sponge into small pieces about 1 × 1 cm ($\frac{1}{2}$ × $\frac{1}{2}$ inch). Place a couple of layers of these over the sauce. Pour the fromage frais over the cake cubes and decorate with the halved grapes. Chill in the fridge for at least 3 hours before serving.

Makes 6 portions. Each portion is 25 g CHO. 165 kcals.

Drinks

Home-made drinks call to mind ladies in woolly hats dispensing their special concoctions at bazaars and fêtes. They cannot compete with mass media images of models in hip-hugging jeans who toss back cans of fizz. These expensive advertising fictions are made to seem more real than the natural substances you keep in the kitchen. Against the commercial propaganda, it can be hard to persuade children in particular that home-made drinks are best. You may achieve some success by involving them in inventing and preparing drinks. At least one of the following recipes was devised, after appropriate trial and error, by my 11-year-old daughter, Naama.

It is hard to grasp the explosive growth in soft drink consumption. Forty years ago, as austerity and rationing ended, Britain drank 634 million litres of fizzy drinks. In 1990, in the throes of another recession, 4,192 million litres were sold in the UK, a sevenfold increase. The annual value of this market is £1,330 million, and it accounts for 25.4 per cent of the sugar used by the food industry.

Fizzy drinks accounted for two thirds of soft drink consumption. They are heavily sweetened. A small can of cola has thirteen lumps of sugar; the diet version has an equivalent of saccharin and aspartame. There are no official restraints in Britain. Only in Mexico are local diet cola drinks marked 'Not recommended for pregnant women and children under seven'.

There are a few harmless manufactured fizzy drinks, usually consisting of a carbonated apple juice base or a mixture of fruit juices and carbonated water. Aqua-libra and Rico are a mixture of juices, herbs and carbonated water. Whole Earth, which has a commitment to producing food without any sugar, has a range of soda drinks, including cola and pink lemonade. These juice-based drinks are, however, high in carbohydrates and contain no fibre – a 250 ml Whole Earth soda contains 27 g CHO. They give an instant boost to blood sugar levels.

The easiest way to make a sugar-free drink is to dilute concentrated or freshly squeezed fruit juice with carbonated water (see pages 80–81). I give only a few recipes in this section for carbonated drinks because the basic principle is easy to grasp and if you have an appreciative audience it is not difficult to build up a wide repertoire based on concentrated juices or puréed fruit. I have focused instead on familiar old drinks, some exotic new ones and on drinks which manage to be both healthy and pleasantly refreshing.

Banana Breakfast Drink

This creamy-smooth high-fibre banana drink will get your day off to a good start. It is gentle on the digestion and provides slow-burning energy in the soluble fibre found in oats.

Bananas have lately been discovered by top athletes as ideal sustenance for endurance sports. Tennis players munch them between games at Wimbledon and the Leeds United winger Gordon Strachan has ascribed his speed and stamina to the high octane fruit. Forget the Lucozade ads. Real speed is peeled from yellow skin.

Bananas have become something of a craze in Japan, where drinks manufacturers are cashing in with some twenty beverages. There is even a banana cola. The drinks are promoted as yuppie fodder. The fanciful English copy on a two-tone yellow can of *Banana au Lait* reads: 'Creative, affluent and rewarding lifestyle. We call this goal Tasteful Living. We are committed to serve the Tasteful Living for everyone's life by various business fields including non-alcoholic beverages.'

400 ml (14 fl oz) cold skimmed milk	bananas
150 g (5 oz) peeled ripe	35 g (1¼ oz generous) porridge oats

Blend the three ingredients well in the liquidizer to make a thick smooth drink. If making it by hand in a screw-top shaker, use ground oats and first sieve the banana before adding to the milk. Serve immediately.

Makes 4 small glasses. Each glass is 20 g CHO. 100 kcals.

If you feel out of sorts pour one large glass (40 g CHO. 200 kcals) for a liquid breakfast.

Barley Tea

This drink is recommended for diabetics in a macrobiotic book called *Diabetes and Hypoglycemia*. The authors argue that too great a reliance on 'extreme yin foods' such as 'white flour, sugar, honey and soft drinks' can contribute to the development of diabetes while too great a reliance on 'extreme yang foods' such as 'meat, poultry, cheese or eggs' can contribute to unstable or chronically low blood glucose or hypoglycaemia. They list foods that are between these two extremes and barley tea is one of them.

The macrobiotic diet takes a great deal from Japanese patterns of eating and cooking, which up until the second half of this century were among the healthiest in the world.

The Japanese are still renowned for their health and longevity, although the incidence of modern chronic diseases has been affected by the growing influence of Western style foods such as hamburgers and steaks.

Barley tea can be bought in instant powdered form requiring only the addition of boiling water. I like to make it from the dry-roasted unhulled barley which can be bought in health food or Japanese shops. The Japanese call it *mugicha*.

2 tbs mugicha   900 ml (1½ pt) water

Spoon the mugicha into the pan of cold water. Bring to the boil and simmer for about 5 minutes, depending on how strong and dark you like it. Strain into cups.

In Japan it is also served iced. Leave to cool and add ice cubes when serving.

(It is possible to dry-roast barley at home. Wash and slowly cook in a frying pan over a medium heat, turning all the while until the grains brown and smell fragrant. It takes very little time but I have to confess to preferring the flavour of the shop-bought variety.)

Makes 4 cups. Negligible CHO and kcals.

Orange-Spiced Tea

An aromatic hot drink that we used to drink in a basement café in Jerusalem. The lights were dim, the voices soft and we sat on large cushions on the floor around low copper tables. The decorations were abstract plaster sculptures made by the café owner, Jan.

600 ml (1 pt) water   2 cinnamon sticks
10 cardamom seeds   10 peppercorns
10 whole cloves

100 g (4 oz) segment of
   orange with peel (use
   organic)

1 tsp tea leaves or 1 tea bag
4 half circles of sliced
   orange with peel

Bring the water to the boil and add the cardamom, cloves, cinnamon sticks, peppercorns and the segment of orange. Simmer gently, covered, for 15 minutes. Remove from the heat and either add tea leaves and strain after a couple of minutes or pour a cup of boiling water over the tea bag and remove 4 tbs tea essence and mix in. I usually make a weak infusion but the strength of the tea is a matter of taste. Serve in two cups with two semi-circles of orange in each.

Makes 2 cups. Negligible CHO and kcals.

Hot Apricot Tea

This and the following drink are ideal if you are not able to eat but only want something light, warm and soothing that will give a small boost to carbohydrate levels.

   Apricot tea is very comforting, especially for anyone with a sore throat. It is based on a recipe I found in an old cookery book. I use apricot jam but there is no reason why it could not be made with blackcurrant or blueberry jam.

50 g (2 oz) sugar-free
   apricot jam
600 ml (1 pt) water

2 tsp lemon juice, freshly
   squeezed

Mix the water and jam in a medium-size pan. Bring to the boil and then simmer, covered, over a low heat for 5 minutes. Sieve well into two cups. Add about 1 teaspoon of lemon juice to each drink according to taste.

Makes 2 cups. Each one is 7.5 g CHO. 35 kcals.

Winter Apple Drink

300 ml (11 fl oz) unsweetened apple juice
150 ml (5 fl oz) water
6 cloves

7.5–10 cm (3–4 inch)
cinnamon stick
1 orange weighing about
150 g (5 oz), quartered

Combine the apple juice, water, cloves, cinnamon stick and quartered orange (including peel) in a medium-sized saucepan. Bring to the boil and simmer, covered, over a gentle heat for 10 minutes. Strain and serve.

Makes 2 cups. Each one is 20 g CHO. 95 kcals.

Lemon Drink

In the winter this is my favourite drink. It is simple to make and refreshing and warming. Resist the temptation to make it with the prepackaged lemon juice – it tastes awful. There is nothing to beat real lemon juice packaged in its own thick skin.

½ lemon (use organic if
available)

boiling water

Wash the lemon and cut it into two slices. Remove any pips. Place them each in a cup and pour enough boiling water on top to make a good-sized drink. Squeeze each piece of lemon with a spoon and leave in the cup. Serve.

Makes 2 drinks. Negligible CHO and kcals.

Hot Carob Drink

The spices mingle very well in this drink. When making it, remember that the milk should not come to the boil as this affects the taste.

4 tbs water	$\frac{1}{4}$ tsp ground cardamom
1 tbs carob powder	400 ml (14 fl oz) skimmed
$\frac{1}{2}$ tsp ground cinnamon	milk or soy milk

Mix the water with the carob powder, cinnamon and cardamom in a small saucepan. Bring to the boil stirring all the time and allow to bubble gently for 1 minute as it thickens. The heat will make the scent of the spices waft around you. Add the milk and heat until it is steaming and a bubble or two have appeared on the side, but do not let it come to the boil. Remove from the heat and serve.

Makes 2 cups. Each cup is 10 g CHO. 75 kcals.

Lemon-Barley Water

This is a traditional tonic drink for anyone who is recovering from an illness but it is also very refreshing and uplifting on a hot summer's day if well chilled. Barley water is recorded as being drunk as early as 1320 and in the eighteenth century George III would refresh himself with this drink as he rode home from hunting.

100 g (4 oz) pot barley	1 lemon, rind peeled, juice strained

Wash the barley. Cover with cold water in a saucepan and bring to the boil and then strain off the water.

Return the barley to the pan with the 1.25 litres (2 pints)

water and the large strips of lemon rind and bring to the boil. Simmer covered over a very low heat for 1 hour. (A heat diffuser can be used over a gas flame to reduce its strength.) Strain the liquid into a jug. It should come to about 600 ml (just under 1 pint). Add the lemon juice. It can be drunk as it is or sweetened with 1–2 tablespoons of apple juice. Chill.

Makes 2 large glasses of lemon-barley water. Each un-sweetened glass in negligible CHO and kcals; sweetened, 5 g CHO. 20 kcals.

Lime Fizz

British sailors in the eighteenth century were known as limeys because of the lime juice issued to them by the Royal Navy to prevent scurvy. Citrus fruits contain vitamin C, which acts as an anti-scorbutic. Attempts were made to reduce the amount of space taken up by citrus fruit in the ship's hold by boiling the juice with sugar. Unfortunately the vitamin C was boiled away in the processing and as sugar contains no nutrients other than calories, the benefic-ial effect was cancelled out.

The best way to serve citrus-based drinks is to cut the fruit when needed and serve immediately.

3 limes   600 ml (1 pt) chilled
                                  carbonated water

Squeeze the juice well from the limes. Add the water and serve immediately.

Serve as it is or garnish with half a slice of lime.

Makes 2 large drinks. Negligible CHO and kcals.

Orange Fizz

This is based on the same principle as Lime Fizz (page 80). Squeeze the juice from an orange and add carbonated water.

300 ml (11 oz) freshly squeezed orange juice (use 2 very large oranges)

500 ml (18 fl oz) carbonated water

Mix the two liquids and serve. Can be garnished with quarter slices of orange.

Makes 4 large drinks. Each drink is 10 g CHO. 30 kcals.

Apricot Nectar Drink

This is a rich health-giving drink. It can be served with ice on a hot day. It is an ideal drink for toddlers as it is packed with vitamin A. If you are making it for little ones try to obtain the unsulphured dried apricots.

150 g (5 oz) dried apricots
600 ml (21 fl oz) spring water

100 ml (4 fl oz) freshly squeezed or unsweetened orange juice

Put the dried apricots with 500 ml (18 fl oz) water in a saucepan and simmer gently until they are softened and about 100 ml (4 fl oz) of liquid is left. Pour this into the liquidizer together with 300 ml of the spring water. Blend to make a thick liquid. Add the orange juice and the remaining spring water. Sieve before storing in the fridge.
   Serve with ice cubes. If too thick, add some cold water.

A 900 ml (1 pt 11 fl oz) jug is 70 g CHO. 310 kcals.

Strawberryade

This recipe provides a concentrated fruit drink which can be diluted with plain or carbonated water according to taste.

450 g (1 lb) strawberries   2 tbs freshly squeezed lime
300 ml (11 fl oz) unsweet-   juice
   ened apple juice

Wash and hull the strawberries. Place them in a medium stainless steel saucepan with the apple and lime juice. Bring to the boil and then simmer for 40 minutes. Sieve the fruit and liquid. It should make about 350 ml (12 fl oz) of concentrated fruit drink. When cool, pour into a jar and store in the fridge where it will keep for a few days.

Makes 8–10 drinks. Each drink is about 5 g CHO. 30 kcals.

Cherryade

Mix this concentrated fruit juice with carbonated water to create your own special fizzy drink. The method of artificially carbonating water was discovered in the late 1760s. At first it was made and sold by chemists but by 1792 Jacob Schweppe had moved to England from Geneva and set up a small factory.

450 g (1 lb) black cherries   150 ml (5 fl oz) unsweet-
                                              ened apple juice

Wash the cherries and pit them. Put them in a pan with the juice and boil vigorously for five minutes so that much of the juice is absorbed. Stir the fruit mixture with a wooden spoon from time to time so that it does not catch on the sides of the pan. Put the fruit mixture through a food mill or sieve.

Leave to cool and then dilute with carbonated water according to taste. Serve with ice cubes and spear a cherry across the top of the glass.

Cherry juice is 60 g CHO. 250 kcals.

Frozen Strawberry Milkshake

350 g (12 oz) strawberries   300 ml (11 oz) skimmed milk

Wash and pat dry the strawberries, hull and slice them and freeze overnight in a freezer bag.

Use the sharp blade of a food processor. Place the frozen strawberries and the milk in the food processor and pulse gently, switching it on and off for short bursts. At first the machine responds jerkily to the frozen fruit, but after a while the fruit breaks into pieces and some of it blends with the milk. The drink can be served like this or if you prefer a smoother texture proceed until no lumps remain.

Makes 2 large drinks. Each drink is 20 g CHO. 95 kcals.

Banana-Carob Milkshake

This milkshake has a very delicate taste.

300 ml (11 fl oz) skimmed   75 g (3 oz) peeled banana
  milk   3 level tsps carob powder

Either pour all the ingredients into a liquidizer and blend, or sieve the banana to a fine liquid and pour with the other ingredients into a screw-top jar and shake until froth appears.

Makes 2 drinks. Each drink is 17.5 g CHO. 90 kcals.

Yogurt Drink

This refreshing and nourishing yogurt drink is found in the hot climates of India and the Middle East. In India it is known as *lassi*, in Iran it is flavoured with fresh mint and called *doogh* and the same drink, further East, is called *tan*.

200 ml (7 fl oz) low-fat
 yogurt

400 ml (14 fl oz) iced water
pinch of salt

Whisk the yogurt, water and salt together. Serve.
    This drink can also be served with a leaf of fresh mint or a pinch of dried mint.

Makes 2 drinks. Each drink is 5 g CHO. 50 kcals.

Mango Yogurt Drink

Since I wrote the recipe for Mango Shortcake in *Sugar-Free Cakes and Biscuits* it has become harder to select a mango because so many different varieties are now imported from all over the world. What you are looking for in the mango flesh is a warm orangey colour, but it is hard to tell from outer skin what lies underneath. A useful tip is to choose a large rather than a small mango because it has had a chance to ripen before being picked. When you touch the skin it should give a little. Fruit skins that are an even yellow or green, or suffused with a reddish glow, all tend to be good omens, while harsh blots of red or black often indicate a fruit that is past its best.

150 g (5 oz) mango
150 g (5 oz) low-fat natural
  yogurt

2 tbs unsweetened apple
  juice
200 ml (7 fl oz) iced water

Blend the mango, yogurt, apple juice and water together to make a smooth drink.

Makes 2 large glasses. Each glass is 10 g CHO. 45 kcals.

Summer Fruit Drink

Hot weather saps the energy and it is important to ensure that one's reserves do not become depleted without realizing it. Enjoy slowly sipping this long, cool, energizing drink made with whole fruit sitting under a sunshade by the edge of the swimming pool.

2 pears weighing about
  250 g (9 oz)
2 nectarines weighing
  about 250 g (9 oz)

2 peaches weighing about
  250 g (9 oz)
2 large oranges weighing
  about 450 g (1 lb)
100 ml (4 fl oz) coconut milk

Wash the pears, nectarines and peaches. Slice all the fruit. Squeeze the juice from the oranges and pour into the liquidizer with the sliced fruit and coconut milk and 100 ml (4 fl oz) water. Blend well until a thick liquid is formed.
  Pour into 4 glasses and top each one with a few ice cubes.

Makes 4 glasses. Each glass is 25 g CHO. 100 kcals.

Pomegranate and Rosewater Drink

This drink comes from Iran, which is famous in the Near and Middle East for the skill of its cooks and the delicacy with which they have created fabulous dishes over the centuries. The taste of this drink is other-worldly and once sipped will never be forgotten.

The pomegranate seeds should be a deep pink-red colour – too pale and there is no taste, too red at the end of their short season and there is very little juice.

2 pomegranates weighing   150 ml (5 fl oz) water
   about 450 g (1 lb)   1 tsp rosewater

The easiest way to remove the juice from the seeds is to use an electric or hand-operated fruit-juice extractor. Wash and dry the pomegranates and cut in half. Place each half on the extractor and bring the lever down firmly. An electric juicer is also very quick to use but involves laborious preparation. All the pomegranate seeds have to be first removed from the rind and also make sure that no pith remains with the seeds as it has a bitter taste due to the high tannin content.

The fruit should make about 150 ml (5 fl oz) liquid. Add at least the same amount of chilled water and the rosewater. You may want to add more depending on how sweet the fruit is. Serve with a few ice cubes.

Makes 2 small glasses. Each glass is 20 g CHO. 75 kcals.

Ices, Sorbets and Festive Ices

Everyone loves ice cream. One thousand million pints of ice cream are consumed annually in the UK. Pour them into pint jugs and lay them end to end and a year's worth of British ices would stretch almost twice around the world. You might thrill to the idea of an ice cream, but it is hard to imagine that anyone would relish the list of ingredients of the most popular brands – frozen sugar and glucose syrup mixed with milk, fat, flour, E numbers and stabilizers.

Even so-called 'natural' ice creams using milk from hand-reared cows and the freshest of fruit, are sweetened with an overdose of sugar and preserved by chemical stabilizers. Make your own and know what you are eating.

Ice cream is not an American invention that spread through Europe with the GIs in the Second World War. It has been eaten around the world for hundreds of years. The Medicis were one of the first European courts to enjoy a regular ice cream treat and by the early seventeenth century the French court was licking 'cream ice'.

The famous eighteenth century English cookery writer Hannah Glasse described how to make ice cream in *The Compleat Confectioner*. Two bowls are fitted inside one another. The outer one contains ice and salt, and the inner one cream and fruit. The mixture is left to freeze, stirred, left to freeze and served. This basic principle has hardly changed. The only modifications introduced are ways of mechanizing the process. The American hand-cranked ice cream freezer invented in 1846 ensured the ice cream mixture was continually moved to prevent ice crystals forming and to add air. Today we have electric commercial and domestic ice cream machines.

Ice Cream Machines

The recipes in this section are quick – the essential factor is how you freeze them. Using the freezer requires no additional outlay but for the best results you will need an ice cream machine. Ice cream machines have not yet forced their way indispensably onto the kitchen worktop between the toaster and the food processor, but they are an incredible boon. The machine converts everything into a cold creamy ice; even without dairy products it still comes out creamy.

State-of-the-art Italian technology provides two options. The Maserati of ice cream machines comes with its own freezing unit. Just plug into the wall and it freezes a mixture in minutes. The Fiat equivalent, cheerful and relatively cheap, comes with a mixing bowl that you keep empty in the freezer for at least 8 hours until it is ready for use. Then remove from the freezer, attach to the machine, and it's a matter of minutes. The walls of the bowl are filled with a liquid chemical solution similar to the kind used in freezer packs. Capacity ranges from $\frac{1}{2}$ to $1\frac{1}{2}$ litres.

Top-of-the-range models cost £250 plus, middle range can be bought for less than £50. A limited variety of makes is available in department stores or specialist kitchen shops. The number has decreased in recent years, because of low demand. Most of the machines are made in Italy although at one time it was possible to buy in England a hand-operated machine made in Japan – always a huge success with children.

That Never-Forgotten Taste

Once you have tasted ice cream that is naturally sweetened with fruit you will never want to insult your taste buds with any other kind. The basic ingredients used in these recipes are fresh fruit, fruit juice and low-fat dairy produce. The reason for using yogurt or fromage frais is that they are light and creamy and contain a fraction of the fat found in double or single cream. Low-fat yogurt contains 1 per cent fat to double cream's 48.2 per cent – and nine times less calories. Yogurts with a slightly higher fat content will provide a richer taste – live yogurt, which has a sweeter taste, contains 3.5 per cent and Greek yogurt contains 10 per cent. Fromage frais is a light cream made of skimmed milk and the amount of fat it contains varies from 1 to 8 per cent.

Yogurt and fromage frais have a much higher water content than cream and for this reason will tend to be icier if left to stand in the freezer. Tofu, made of soy beans, is an ideal alternative for vegans or anyone avoiding milk in their diet. It contains only 5 per cent fat and can be substituted for yogurt or fromage frais in the fruit ice recipes. If you wrap it in a tea towel and put a heavy weight on it to remove water before using you will find it gives bulk and form to fruit ices. Egg yolks and skimmed milk are used to make a traditional custard base. It is a useful method if you are not using an ice cream machine because it improves the texture and gives a richer flavour. Be sure to use eggs that come from a reliable uninfected source as they are only partially cooked in this method.

Recipes in this chapter for Sorbets begin on page 102, and starting on page 110 is a selection of recipes for festive ice cream concoctions for parties and other special occasions.

Alternatives to Cream: How They Compare

	FAT (per cent)	WATER (per cent)	CALORIES (per 100 g)
Double cream	48.2	48.6	447
Single cream	21.2	71.9	212
Natural low-fat yogurt	1.0	85.7	52
Fromage frais	7.0	78	113
	(ranges 1–8%)		
Firm tofu	5.3	84.8	87

Sources: McCance and Widdowson, *The Composition of Foods*; Shurtleff and Aoyagi, *The Book of Tofu*.

Clementine-Banana Ice

This soft creamy ice is made with frozen fruit and yogurt in a food processor. In some cafés you can buy an ice made from frozen fruit and frozen yogurt – recently we were thrilled to find a snack bar selling what it claimed were sugar-free ices. Closer inspection, however, revealed the yogurt to be sweetened with sugar and isomalt. The manufacturers maintain that the yogurt will not freeze properly without sugar – but I get a successful result by using chilled unsweetened yogurt.

150 g (5 oz) peeled bananas
2 clementines weighing
   about 175 g (6 oz)

100 ml (4 fl oz) low-fat
   natural yogurt or live
   yogurt, chilled

Cut the bananas into thin slices, place them in a freezer bag and freeze until hard. Peel the clementines, remove any pith, break into segments and also freeze until hard.

Use the sharp blade of a food processor. Place the frozen fruit and chilled yogurt in the processor and switch it on and off for short bursts. Initially the processor responds jerkily to the hard fruit but after a while the fruit is converted into a thick, delicate-flavoured cream.

Makes 4 servings. Each serving is 10 g CHO. 50 kcals.

Quick Banana Ice Cream

Research into smells and their effects by the Catholic University in Washington revealed that the fragrance of vanilla decreases stress. Banana contains food compounds similar to those found in vanilla, so you should find this ice very relaxing.

300 g (11 oz) peeled ripe
  banana
150 g (5 oz) low-fat yogurt,
  live yogurt or fromage
  frais

100 ml (4 fl oz) unsweet-
  ened apple juice
1 tsp vanilla essence

Either blend all the ingredients in a liquidizer or, if making by hand, use a sieve or food mill to purée the banana. Then stir in the yogurt, apple juice and vanilla essence. Chill before pouring into the ice cream machine and then follow the manufacturer's instructions. If freezing in the freezer leave for about 45 minutes, until frozen around the edges. Remove and whisk to break up the ice crystals and return to the freezer. Repeat once more.

Makes 4 portions. Each portion is 20 g CHO. 90 kcals.

Banana-Cherry Ice Cream

During a recent June, when it was sizzling hot every afternoon, I would take down the blender and ice cream machine from the cupboard and quickly throw together this unusual fruit combination before the girls came home from school. We had it every day but no one was ever bored.

At the beginning of the cherry season I had a lot of trouble finding sweet tasting cherries. They would look reasonable but have no taste at all, regardless of the price. The Turkish and Italian cherries had the most flavour – they were less puffed up than the Spanish and American varieties and their taste was denser and less watery. The only satisfactory method of knowing which cherries to choose is to try one.

1 recipe Banana Ice Cream using live yogurt or	fromage frais (page 91) 125 g (4½ oz) cherries

Mix the banana ice cream ingredients according to the instructions.

Wash, dry and slice the cherries. Stir them into the banana ice cream mixture. Chill before pouring into the ice cream machine and then follow the manufacturer's instructions.

If freezing in the freezer leave for about 45 minutes until frozen around the edges. Remove and whisk to break up the ice crystals and return to the freezer. Repeat once more and then leave to harden.

Makes 4 generous portions. Each portion is 20 g CHO. 102 kcals.

Blackberry Ice Cream

It is important to use very ripe pears for this ice cream because they contribute a sweet background to the blackberries. When fruit is frozen its sweet taste is slightly dulled.

350 g (12 oz) ripe pears 300 g (11 oz) blackberries 150 ml (5 fl oz) unsweetened apple juice	150 ml (5 fl oz) low-fat or live yogurt or fromage frais

Wash and dry the pears and blackberries. Pick out 75–100 g (3–4 oz) blackberries, place on a freezer tray and freeze to use as a garnish. Slice the pears with the skin on and blend in the liquidizer with the remaining blackberries and apple juice. To remove the blackberry seeds either sieve or grind through a hand food mill. Stir in the yogurt.

Pour the fruit purée into the ice cream machine and follow the manufacturer's instructions. If you are using a freezer, remove the covered container when the sides have become frozen and whisk to break up the ice crystals. Repeat this once more and then leave to set.

Serve each helping with four or five of the frozen blackberries on top.

Makes 6 servings. Each serving is 10 g CHO. 50 kcals.

Strawberry Ice Cream

Strawberries are not only scrumptious but also nutritious. The cultivated garden variety is higher in vitamin C than oranges – up to 90 mg per 100 grams compared to 60 mg for oranges – while wild strawberries contain even more!

If you can afford organic strawberries or grow your own you will find that they give the sweetest taste to this ice cream.

550 g (1 lb 4 oz) ripe strawberries
75 g (3 oz) dried dates
150 ml (5 fl oz) unsweet-
ened apple juice

100 ml (4 fl oz) freshly
squeezed or unsweet-
ened orange juice
150 ml (5 fl oz) low-fat live
yogurt or fromage frais

Wash and hull the strawberries. Finely chop 100 g (4 oz) of them and set aside. Put the dates in a pan with the orange and apple juice and cook on a medium heat briefly until the dates can be mashed with a fork in the juice. A good deal of the juice should remain in the saucepan. Blend the remaining strawberries, yogurt and date paste in the liquidizer. Cool in the fridge. Just before pouring into the ice cream machine add the reserved finely chopped strawberries.

If freezing the ice cream in the freezer, cover the container and remove after 45–60 minutes and whisk to break up the ice crystals. Return to the freezer and repeat this process once more taking care not to mash the strawberry pieces. Ideally serve when the ice has become solid. If prepared in advance remove from the freezer about 30 minutes before serving.

Makes 6 portions. Each portion is 20 g CHO. 85 kcals.

Mango Ice Cream

This is the come-back-and-ask-for more variety of creamy ice cream. It is successful because ripe mangoes are deliciously sweet and their fibrous nature gives a good texture. The best way to remove the flesh is to peel the mango all over and, using a sharp knife, cut slices lengthways so that only the stone remains.

500 g (1 lb 2 oz) ripe mango, without the skin or stones

100 ml (4 fl oz) unsweetened apple juice
150 g (5 oz) Greek yogurt or firm tofu

Slice the mango. Place it in a liquidizer with the apple juice and yogurt and blend to make a thick purée.

Chill and pour into the ice cream machine and follow the manufacturer's instructions. If using the freezer, cover the container and remove after 45 minutes when the ice cream has begun to turn to ice at the sides, and whisk. Return to the freezer. Repeat this process once more. Either serve when it has set firm or, if prepared the day before, remove from the freezer about 30 minutes before serving.

Makes 4 portions. Each portion is 25 g CHO. 135 kcals.

Frutti Ice Cream

A tantalizing mixture of fresh fruits in creamy ice.

125 g (4½ oz) fromage frais
75 g (3 oz) peeled banana
75 g (3 oz) fresh dates, stoned
50 ml (2 fl oz) unsweetened apple juice
50 g (2 oz) hulled strawberries
1 small kiwi
50 g (2 oz) orange segments
50 g (2 oz) yellow plum

Blend the fromage frais, banana, dates and apple juice to make a thick cream. While it is chilling in the refrigerator, chop the strawberries, kiwi, orange and plum into small pieces. Combine the cream and fruit and pour into the ice cream machine and follow the manufacturer's instructions. If freezing in the freezer, stir after 45 minutes but take care not to mash the chopped fruit.

This ice should be served frozen hard. When it is set firm, scoop balls of the ice cream on to a tray, cover and return to the freezer.

Makes 4 portions. Each portion is 15 g CHO. 80 kcals.

Black Cherry Ice Cream

This recipe makes a deep purple, mouthwatering ice.

450 g (1 lb) black cherries
250 ml (8 fl oz) unsweet-
    ened apple juice

150 g (5 oz) Greek yogurt
    or firm tofu

Wash and stone the cherries. Put the cherries and apple juice in a liquidizer and whizz for a few seconds to make a thin liquid. Pour this into a saucepan, bring to the boil and, reducing the heat to low, simmer until the liquid has thickened and measures about 500 ml (16 fl oz).

When the fruit mixture has cooled, whisk in the yogurt. Pour the chilled mixture into the ice cream machine and follow the manufacturer's instructions. Alternatively freeze, covered, in the freezer, removing twice to whisk and break up the ice crystals as much as possible.

Makes 4 large portions. Each portion is 20 g CHO. 125 kcals.

Raspberry Cream Lollies

My daughters love this special treat. As well as using the mixture to make lollies you could use it as a basis for a quick fancy dessert – set the mixture in ice cube trays and serve a few squares on each plate with a coulis made of liquidized tinned raspberries in natural juice. For a dairy-free version use coconut milk instead of fromage frais.

100 ml (4 fl oz) low-fat fro-
    mage frais
100 g (4 oz) peeled banana

250 g (9 oz) frozen rasp-
    berries

Choose the moulds for the lollies and lay them out ready.

Mash the banana well with a fork until it becomes almost smooth. Add to the fromage frais. Remove the raspberries from the freezer and stir briskly into the fromage frais mixture. Spoon quickly into the moulds before the raspberries thaw and become soft. The colder the raspberries are the quicker the lollies set. You may need to press the mixture down well with a teaspoon.

Leave to set in the freezer. Setting time depends on the size of the lollies. If you are using an ice cube tray divided into squares, an hour and a half should be adequate for them to become rock hard. Moulds on a stick can require a little longer to make sure they do not become detached from the stick when removed.

Makes 6 large lollies. Each lolly is 5 g CHO. 30 kcals.

Carob Ice Cream

Britons are top of the list with the Swiss as the biggest eaters of chocolate in the world. Chocolate in its natural state is bitter and has sugar and fat added to make it into a chocolate bar. Carob does not have the same taste but has the advantage of being naturally sweet. It also does not contain caffeine and theobromine, which can become addictive, or phenethylamine and tyramine, which can cause migraine.

Decorate this rich creamy ice with violet petals. Use the wild purple violets that grow in the spring. The petals should be washed and dried before using.

150 g (5 oz) carob bar, broken in pieces
2 egg yolks
2 tsp arrowroot

450 ml (15 fl oz) skimmed milk
150 g (5 oz) peeled banana

Melt the carob bar in a bowl standing in a saucepan of shallow simmering water. Be careful that no water gets into the bowl.

While the carob is melting, whisk the egg yolks and arrowroot together. Bring the milk to just below boiling point – when bubbles appear on the sides remove from the heat. Pour over the egg yolks, stirring. Return to a heavy thick-based saucepan and stir continuously with a wooden spoon over very low heat until the mixture thickens and coats the back of the spoon. Add the melted carob to make a smooth dark brown mixture. Take off the heat and add the finely mashed banana.

Blend all the ingredients in a food processor or liquidizer. Chill. Pour into an ice cream machine and follow the manufacturer's instructions or freeze in the freezer.

Makes 6 portions. Each portion is 20 g CHO. 200 kcals.

Apricot Ice Cream

This is a lovely rich creamy ice bursting with vitamin A and generously laced with minerals. The apricot is a remarkable fruit from the health point of view and it is not surprising that the Hunzas who live in the foothills of the Himalayas and in whose diet the apricot plays a large part are renowned for their good health. A portion of dried apricots contains more iron and magnesium than most cuts of meat, almost as much phosphorus and three-quarters as much calcium as milk.

150 g (5 oz) dried apricots
2 egg yolks
1½ tsp arrowroot

350 ml (12 fl oz) skimmed milk
100 ml (4 fl oz) unsweetened apple juice

Cover the dried apricots with water and simmer over a low heat until a couple of tablespoons of liquid remain. Blend in the liquidizer or processor to a smooth paste.

Whisk the egg yolks with the arrowroot. Heat the milk to just below boiling point. Pour it slowly over the yolks, stirring. Return the mixture to a heavy thick-based pan. Stir continuously with a wooden spoon over very low heat until the mixture thickens and coats the back of the spoon. Remove from the heat and stir in the apricot purée and apple juice.

Cool. Chill in the refrigerator before pouring into the ice cream machine. If freezing in the freezer remove the covered container and whisk three times while it is setting.

Makes 4 portions. Each portion is 25 g CHO. 140 kcals.

Pistachio-Cardamom Ice Cream

This fragrant ice cream has a hint of cardamom spice. The amount specified in the recipe is only a guideline and it is useful to taste the custard base from time to time to check that the flavour is to your liking.

Cardamom is a south Indian herb and is used in the Middle East to flavour coffee. It is said that if the pod and seed are chewed it sweetens the breath and can disguise the smell of garlic.

2 egg yolks
2 rounded tsps arrowroot
450 ml (15 fl oz) skimmed milk
$\frac{1}{8}$–$\frac{1}{4}$ tsp ground cardamom
200 g (7 oz) peeled banana, sieved
1 tbs rosewater

100 ml (4 fl oz) unsweetened apple juice
few drops of green colouring (optional)
60 g (2 oz generous) shelled pistachio nuts (not salted)

Whisk the egg yolks with the arrowroot. Heat the milk and cardamom to just below boiling point. Pour it slowly over the yolks, stirring. Return the mixture to a heavy based pan. Stir continuously with a wooden spoon over a very low heat until the mixture thickens and coats the back of the spoon.

Remove from the heat and stir in the liquid banana. Add the rosewater, apple juice and green colouring, if using, and leave to cool.

Chop the nuts and add to the mixture when it is cold. Pour into the ice cream machine and follow the manufacturer's instructions. If using the freezer, cover the container and remove after about 45 minutes when the ice cream has begun to turn to ice at the sides and whisk to break up the ice crystals. Return to the freezer. Repeat this process twice more. Either serve when it has set firm or if prepared the day before remove from the freezer about 30 minutes before serving.

Makes 4 portions. Each portion is 20 g CHO. 215 kcals.

Cinnamon Ice Cream

This is a great favourite with everyone. Crushed cinnamon balls are mixed with a creamy ice to make an unusual spiced ice cream, and served with whole cinnamon balls dipped in coconut.

Cinnamon balls
75 g (3 oz) dried dates
150 ml (5 fl oz) water
100 g (4 oz) ground
   almonds

15 g (½ oz) ground oats
2 tsps ground cinnamon
1 egg white
desiccated coconut

Ice cream
1 egg yolk
1 rounded tsp arrowroot
200 ml (7 fl oz) skimmed
  milk

75 g (3 oz) peeled ripe
  banana, sieved
200 ml (7 fl oz) low-fat
  fromage frais
few drops of vanilla
  essence

Prepare the cinnamon balls: put the dried dates in a pan with the water and simmer on a low light until all the water is absorbed and it is possible to mash the dates to a purée with a fork. Blend in a small food processor or coffee grinder to a smooth paste.

Combine the ground almonds, oats and cinnamon. Mix in the date paste. Whisk the egg white until it forms stiff peaks and fold in.

Moisten the palms of your hands with cold water and roll the cinnamon mixture into small balls. Place them on a greased baking sheet and bake slowly in a preheated oven (gas mark 3/325°F/170°C) for about 25 minutes, until they begin to brown lightly on the outside and turn brown underneath. After removing from the oven roll half the warm cinnamon balls in desiccated cocount. Leave to cool. These can be prepared the day before.

Prepare the ice cream by making a simple custard with the egg yolk and milk. Lightly beat the egg yolk and arrowroot with a fork. Heat the milk in a small saucepan to just below boiling point. Pour over the yolk and arrowroot, stirring. Pour the mixture back into the pan and cook on a very low heat, stirring continuously with a wooden spoon, until the mixture thickens and coats the back of the spoon.

When the custard has thickened pour it into a bowl and add the liquid banana which has been sieved or put through a food mill. Stir in the fromage frais and vanilla essence. Leave to cool.

Break the cinnamon balls not rolled in dessicated coconut

into very small pieces and add to the cream mixture. Stir well and pour into a freezer container. Cover and leave to freeze for about 3 hours until the ice cream firms, stirring once during this time. The length of time is only a rough guideline as all freezers are different. If the ice cream is prepared the day before remove from the freezer thirty minutes before serving so that it is not rock hard. Like all the other ice cream recipes it tastes best when made with an ice cream machine. Decorate each serving with a few cinnamon balls.

Makes 4 large servings of ice cream with the cinnamon balls. Each serving is 25 g CHO. 290 kcals.

Sorbets

Fruit sorbets are fruit ices made without any milk, yogurt or cream. The traditional and complicated way of making a sorbet is with sugar syrup and raw egg whites. The syrup sweetens and the egg whites are meant to give a firmer consistency; but these ingredients are not essential when you sweeten with fruit. Fruits are blended together and either frozen in the freezer or, for the best results, mixed in an ice cream sorbet maker. Raw egg white can be added but there is no particular need for it. If you do use egg in a recipe be sure that it comes from a reliable uninfected source.

Mango Sorbet

A fruit ice requires top-quality fruit because that is the source of its flavour. Mangoes are imported from different countries into Britain and each variety looks slightly different when it is ripe, so it can be quite difficult to make a selection. The tastiest are often large ones with an even coloured orangey-yellow, green or red tinted skin that gives a little to the touch, rather than the ones which have fierce contrasting colours.

Mangoes contain more carotene than the other tropical fruits used in this book – 1800 micrograms per 100 grams. Mangoes are also a useful source of vitamin C – containing four times as much as apples.

400 g (14 oz) mango flesh, either 1 very large mango or 2 medium ones

1 ripe pear weighing about 150 g (5 oz), peeled
1 tbs freshly squeezed lemon juice

Blend the mango, pear and lemon juice to make a thick fruit purée. If using an ice-cream machine follow the manufacturer's instructions. If freezing in a freezer container remove after about 45 minutes when the sides have become icy and whisk the mixture. Remove every 45 minutes and whisk to break up the ice crystals. Depending on the coldness of the freezer it should take 2½–3 hours to become firm enough to serve.

Makes 4 large portions. Each portion is 20 g CHO. 70 kcals.

Kiwi Sorbet with Cape Gooseberries

A delicious treat from the Antipodes. Be careful when choosing the ripe kiwis: they should be firm not soft and when the fruit is cut open it should be a light grass green.

Serve this ice with Cape gooseberries or, as they are also called, Physalis. You have probably seen them in the supermarket or greengrocer – they look like miniature Chinese lanterns and have a delicate ethereal beauty. The paper thin husk surrounds a golden orange berry. The berries can be kept for a number of weeks as long as they are left in their husks. They appear in the shops in the winter months. The berries are a natural diuretic – that is they cause the body to pass more water than usual – and contain carotene and small amounts of niacin and iron.

6 large kiwis weighing about 450–475 g (1 lb–1 lb 1 oz)
100 g (4 oz) peeled ripe banana

150 ml (5 fl oz) unsweet-ened apple juice
16 Cape goosberries

Peel the kiwis and place in the blender. Add the banana and apple juice and whizz for a few seconds until smooth. If using an ice-cream machine switch on and pour in the liquid. If freezing in the freezer place in a covered container and leave for 45 minutes until the sorbet is frozen around the edges. Remove and whisk then return to the freezer. Repeat this process once more. The reason for doing it is to avoid large ice crystals developing.

Serve in scoops surrounded by the Cape gooseberries.

Makes 4 servings. Each serving is 20 g CHO. 100 kcals.

Watermelon Sorbet

The watermelon should be chosen with care. It should be ripe for eating. Some people test them by tapping the outside and listening to the reverberations. If you have a good greengrocer ask his advice.

900 g (2 lbs) watermelon
75 g (3 oz) dried dates
100 ml (4 fl oz) water

1 tbs lime juice, freshly squeezed

Cut the watermelon off the rind and remove the seeds. Do this over a large bowl or plate so that none of the juice is lost.

Put the dates and water in a small pan. Heat over a low light until the water has been absorbed and the dates can be mashed to a purée with a fork.

Spoon the watermelon, date purée and lime juice into the liquidizer and whizz to make a thin liquid. Chill in the fridge and then pour into the ice cream machine. If it is being set in the freezer, remove the covered container after one hour, whisk and then leave to harden.

Makes 4 portions. Each portion is 20 g CHO. 70 kcals.

White Melon Sorbet

A simple sorbet that provides a light ending to a meal. If you want to make it look like an entry for the television cookery competition *Masterchef*, surround the sorbet with fresh balls of melon, either the same variety or for a contrasting colour, use cantaloupe.

Use a melon that is ripe and ready to eat. Avoid underripe melons because they are not sweet enough and the overripe ones have an unpleasant taste. The amount of apple juice that is added depends on the sweetness of the melon.

950 g (2 lb 2 oz) galia melon, weighed with the rind but without the seeds

3–4 tbs unsweetened apple juice

Remove the melon from the rind and put in a blender with the apple juice. Whizz for a few seconds to make a sweet liquid. Chill.

Either put in the ice cream machine and follow the manufacturer's instructions or put covered in the freezer, for about 2–3 hours, removing every 45 minutes to whisk and break down the ice crystals.

Makes 4 portions of melon ice. Each portion is 10 g CHO. 35 kcals.

Orange Sorbet

Oranges are famous for their vitamin C content but it requires careful cherishing. If you like your orange juice hot the heat will have destroyed much of the beneficial vitamin C, while more than 30 minutes exposure to air, or in other words oxygen, will reduce it by 50 per cent. Oranges are high in pectin, a type of soluble fibre – a medium-sized orange contains over 2 g. Pectin helps to reduce high blood cholesterol levels.

75 g (3 oz) dried dates
150 ml (5 fl oz) water
3 oranges weighing about 600 g (1 lb 5 oz)
1 tbs freshly squeezed or

unsweetened orange juice
1 level tsp orange zest (use an organic orange)

Put the dates in a pan with the water and simmer on a low heat until the dates can be mashed with a fork to make a thick paste. Peel the oranges and remove the pith and pips. Place the orange in the blender with the mashed dates, orange juice and zest and whizz for a few seconds to make a thick liquid. Either sieve or put the liquid through a food mill. If you don't do this it will still taste delicious but will be unusually fibrous for an ice.

Allow the mixture to cool and pour it into the ice cream machine and follow the manufacturer's instructions. If using the freezer, cover the container and remove after about 45 minutes when the ice has begun to ice up at the sides and whisk to break up the ice crystals. Return to the freezer and leave to set firm. Remove from the freezer half an hour before serving.

Serve garnished with a mint leaf. For a more elaborate presentation, cut the three oranges in half, remove the flesh and freeze the empty peels until firm. To serve, fill the peels with the orange sorbet. Round the tops of the ice with a spoon. Return, covered, to the freezer until needed.

Makes 6 servings. Each serving is 15 g CHO. 60 kcals.

Raspberry and Rosewater Sorbet

This is a delicate perfumed ice that has a deep red hue. It can be served by itself or piped on to individual portions of fruit salad.

Rosewater is distilled from roses. It gives a perfumed sweetness to any dish that it is added to but should be used in moderation or it takes on a soapy taste. A description of how it used to be made in Iraq is found in a book called *The Best of Baghdad Cooking* by Daisy Iny: 'We used to buy *warid joory* (a light-pink wild rose) in great quantities of twenty kilos or more. The roses were put in a huge copper pot with a wide bottom and narrower opening at the top. The roses were covered with water and the pot was placed on a low wood fire to cook. A small cane pipe was secured to an opening in the lid with clay. A series of connecting pipes carried the steam away and through a basin of cold water on the floor until the condensation dripped into clean glass bottles. There was an inch or more of oil topping the first few bottles which contained rosewater with the strongest flavour.'

450 g (1 lb) fresh raspberries
100 g (4 oz) ripe peeled
banana, mashed

2 tbs rosewater
50 ml (2 fl oz) unsweetened
apple juice

Sieve the raspberries and mashed banana through a food
mill. This removes the raspberry seeds and reduces the
banana to a liquid consistency. Stir in the apple juice and
rosewater. Chill in the refrigerator.

Either pour the cooled liquid into an ice cream maker or
put it, covered, in the freezer, whisking it every 45 minutes
until it is set firm and ready to serve.

Makes 4 portions. Each portion is 12.5 g CHO. 55 kcals.

Lemon Sorbet

This ice is exquisitely pungent. Since lemon is so sharp it
requires a lot of natural sweetener to make it as sweet as
comparative ices. This increases the carbohydrate level so it
is best to make this ice in small quantities and use it as a
decorative garnish for desserts rather than as the main part.
Many people prefer their lemon sorbet sour and if you are
one of them reduce the amount of dried dates to 50 g (2 oz).
This will reduce each portion to 10 g CHO.

2 lemons weighing about
200 g (7 oz)
100 g (4 oz) dried dates
100 ml (4 fl oz) water

100 ml (4 fl oz) unsweet-
ened apple juice
$\frac{1}{4}$ tsp lemon zest (use
organic lemon)

Put the dried dates in a saucepan with the water and
simmer on a low heat until the water has been absorbed.
Mash the dates to a paste. Leave to cool.

Peel the lemons and remove the pips and pith. Put the

flesh in the blender together with the date paste, apple juice and lemon zest. If you are using an ice cream machine follow the manufacturer's instructions. Otherwise put in a freezer container, remove every 45 minutes to whisk the sorbet and stop too large ice crystals forming, for 2–3 hours. This sorbet has a lovely firm texture.

Provides enough decoration for 6 desserts. Each portion is 15 g CHO. 55 kcals.

Passionfruit and Pear Sorbet

This is a scrumptuous ice cream with a smooth taste. It goes very well with raspberry tart. Passionfruit have the same smell as berries that grow wild in the woods and when combined with ripe pears make a very successful sorbet. Surprisingly they are very low in carbohydrates – one pound is equivalent to 16 grams of carbohydrate.

650 g (1 lb 7 oz) ripe pears
4 tbs of passionfruit flesh
  (about 5 small passion
  fruits)

100 ml (4 fl oz) unsweet-
  ened apple juice

Peel the pears and slice them, then put into the liquidizer. Pour in the apple juice and blend. The sliced pears could also be liquidized through a hand-operated food mill. Stir in the passionfruit pulp and either pour into a freezer container or use an ice cream machine. If using the freezer remove the ice every 45 minutes and whisk it around to break up the large ice crystals. It will take about 3 hours to become firm. If using an ice cream machine follow the manufacturer's instructions.

Makes 4 large servings. Each serving is 15 g CHO. 65 kcals.

Festive Ices

Ices can be put together in different combinations to make glorious desserts for special occasions or just a real treat! Here are a few ideas.

Knickerbocker Glory

A splendid finale to any party – layers of fruit, sauce, nuts and ice cream. Whet your guests' appetites by making this knock-out dessert at the serving table in the same way that Italian ice cream parlours create a magnificent concoction in front of your marvelling eyes.

1 recipe Quick Banana Ice
    Cream (page 91)

1 eating apple weighing
    about 150 g (5 oz), or
    200 g (7 oz) strawberries
100 g (4 oz) green grapes
75 g (3 oz) fresh dates

25–40 g (1–1½ oz) finely
    chopped walnuts or
    flaked almonds

Raspberry Sauce
300 g (11 oz) raspberries
50 ml (2 fl oz) unsweetened
    apple juice

First, prepare the ice cream and leave it to freeze or prepare in the ice cream machine.

Dice the apple. Cut the grapes in half. Remove the skin from the dates and chop up small, mixing together with the other fruit. Store covered in the fridge.

Prepare the sauce: put the raspberries in a pan with the apple juice. Bring to the boil and simmer for half a minute. Taste for sweetness; add extra apple juice if necessary. Remove from the heat and sieve or put through a food mill to remove the seeds. Leave to cool.

To assemble the dessert, use four tall glasses on a stem – seeing the different layers is part of the pleasure of this recipe. Spoon half the fruit into the base of the glasses. Cover with a little raspberry sauce. Follow with a thin layer of ice cream. Repeat the fruit layer and sprinkle with nuts before pouring the raspberry sauce on top. Cover again with the remaining ice cream and top with the nuts and some swirls of sauce. (If your serving glasses are narrow it is possible to make three layers of ice cream and fruit.)

Makes 4 servings. Each serving is 40 g CHO. 210 kcals.

Neapolitan Profiteroles

Choux paste puffs filled with ice cream and served with two sauces, one pink and one brown, make a sensational dessert.
  Don't be intimidated by the idea of choux pastry – it is quite simple to make. The main concern is that it should puff up and that has more to do with getting the right oven temperature than any culinary skill. The recipe recommends gas 6/400°F/200°C but if by the end of the first 10–15 minutes the puffs have not risen, increase the heat to gas 7/425°F/210°C for a few minutes until the desired effect is achieved and then reduce the heat for the remainder of the cooking time.

Choux paste
75 g (3 oz) wholewheat
  flour
150 ml (5 fl oz) water
40 g (1½ oz) margarine
2 large eggs

Ice cream filling
1 quantity Quick Banana
  Ice Cream (page 91)
100 g (4 oz) strawberries

Pink sauce
2 oranges weighing about
  150 g (5 oz) each
300 g (11 oz) strawberries,
  washed and hulled

Carob-pear sauce
600 g (1 lb 5 oz) ripe pears
1½ tbs unsweetened apple
  juice
75 g (3 oz) carob bar

For the choux paste: Sift the flour into a bowl. Put the water and margarine into a medium saucepan. Slowly heat the pan until the margarine has melted, then bring to the boil and when the water and margarine are bubbling remove the pan from the heat. Once the bubbles have gone down pour in all the flour and stir vigorously with a wooden spoon for a few seconds until a smooth paste is formed. Leave to cool for about five minutes.

Whisk the eggs very lightly with a fork. Do not add all the egg to the flour mixture at once – add in about three stages. The finished paste should keep its shape and be firm so you may not need to add all the egg. Beat the pastry with a wooden spoon for a few minutes until it is smooth and shiny.

Choux pastry is baked on a dampened baking tray – hold the tray under the cold tap for a few seconds. Put 16–18 teaspoonfuls of the pastry on the tray. It is surprising how much they will rise. Bake in a preheated oven (gas 6/400°F/ 200°C) for 25–30 minutes. Bake until brown and firm to the touch.

Remove the profiteroles from the baking tray using a spatula. Make a small hole with the point of a knife in the side of each one to release any steam. This keeps them crisp. Leave to cool.

To make the ice cream filling: Chop the washed, dried and hulled strawberries and stir them into the banana ice cream mixture. Either put the ice cream in a machine and follow the manufacturer's instructions or put in the freezer in a special container. If using the latter method remove the ice cream just before it is set solid so that it can still be easily scooped in a spoon (about 2 hours, but this does depend on the depth of the ice cream container and the type of freezer you use).

Spoon the ice cream into the profiteroles, generously

filling them so that one side is wide open with pink ice cream. Place in a covered container in the freezer to firm. Put a sheet of greaseproof paper between the layers. The profiteroles should be filled on the day they are made but they can be served the next day. When left overnight remove from the freezer for 15–30 minutes before serving otherwise the ice cream will be rock hard.

To make the pink sauce: Peel the oranges and remove all the pith and pips. Put the segments in a blender or food processor together with the strawberries to make a fruit purée. Sieve this into a saucepan and bring to the boil, then remove from the heat. Serve either warm or cold.

For the carob-pear sauce: The ripe pears will be quite soft and when chopped up with their skins will blend easily with the apple juice to make a thick smooth liquid. Pour this into a medium sized pan and slowly heat. Break up the carob bar into the pan and stir with a wooden spoon while it slowly melts. This is a very thick sauce and is most delicious served hot.

Assemble the dessert: On a flat plate put a generous tablespoon of the pink sauce and one of the hot brown sauce side by side. Place the profiteroles so that they just touch the tip of the two sauces.

This recipe provides 8 servings of two profiteroles per person plus sauce. Each serving is 30 g CHO. 220 kcals.

Baked Alaska

In the 1950s ice cream baked on a sponge base and encircled with meringue was a very fashionable dessert. When my mother used to whisk it out of her oven it would invariably cause a sensation. As I already suspected her of possessing magical powers I was not entirely astonished. Beaten egg white is a poor conductor of heat, so the ice cream emerges from the hot oven still frozen solid.

This recipe goes back rather further than the 1950s – the French claim it first appeared in the 1860s when, according to the *Larousse Gastronomique*, a visiting Chinese chef showed the chefs at the Grand Hotel in Paris the 'art of cooking vanilla and ginger ices in the oven'. The Americans say it was created in 1867 to celebrate Alaska joining the Union.

This version is made without any milk products and all of it, except for the meringue, can be prepared in advance.

Cake base
50 g (2 oz) dried dates
100 ml (4 fl oz) water
75 g (3 oz) peeled ripe banana
2 eggs, separated
40 g (1½ oz) wholewheat flour

Raspberry Ice
350 g (12 oz) tin of raspberries in unsweetened apple juice

3 ripe pears weighing about 375 g (13 oz)

Meringue
3 egg whites
100 g (4 oz) ripe banana, peeled

Fruit
450 g (1 lb) strawberries (in winter use 4 ripe persimmons), thinly sliced
3 tbs unsweetened apple juice

For the cake base: Grease and flour the base and sides of a 20 cm (8 inch) diameter baking tin. Heat the dates and the water in a small pan until the water is absorbed. Blend in a processor with the banana.

Whisk the egg yolks until pale and creamy. Add the date and banana mixture. Whisk the egg whites stiffly and fold in. Gently fold in the flour.

Pour the mixture into the prepared dish and bake in a preheated oven (gas 5/375°F/190°C) for 10 minutes, until the surface is lightly browned. Remove and leave to cool.

Prepare the raspberry ice: Wash and dry the pears. Remove any blemished skin and slice into the liquidizer. Add the raspberries and their juice and whizz for a few seconds into a fruit purée. Sieve to remove the seeds. Either pour the chilled liquid in an ice cream machine and follow the manufacturer's instruction or place in a covered container in the freezer, removing to whisk a couple of times before it finally sets hard.

The ice cream will eventually be spread over the surface of the sponge. An attractive alternative is to make it into eight balls or rounds and leave to harden on a sheet of parchment paper in a chilled covered container in the freezer until needed.

Prepare the meringue: Put the banana through a food mill or sieve. (If using a metal sieve make sure it is very clean because they sometimes give a greyish colour to the banana). Whisk the egg whites very stiffly into peaks and fold in the banana.

Assemble the Baked Alaska: Place the cake on a 25 cm (10 inch) diameter baking dish. Spread the ice cream or place the scoops on top, leaving a margin of sponge around the outside. Pour the meringue over the ice cream ensuring that it is completely covered at the sides. Bake in the top half of a preheated oven (gas 6/400°F/200°C) for four to five minutes, until the meringue has turned golden.

While it is baking, heat the strawberries in a pan with the apple juice and simmer for 1 minute.

Serve the Baked Alaska as soon as it is removed from the oven with the hot fruit.

Makes 8 servings. Each serving is 20 g CHO. 115 kcals.

La Bombe

A *bombe* is an ice cream in an inverted pudding shape which consists of at least two layers of ice cream. This one is made with mango and banana ice cream. If you do not have the right shape mould use a square plastic container – it will still result in a deliciously mouthwatering dessert.

1 recipe Mango Ice Cream   25 g (1 oz) dried apricot,
   (page 94)   chopped finely
1 recipe Quick Banana Ice
   Cream (page 91)

If the mould is first covered in parchment paper it will be easier to remove the bombe. Flatten the paper well against the sides because any creases will mark the ice cream surface.

Prepare the mango ice cream according to the instructions. It is easier to use in this recipe if it is prepared in an ice cream machine. If you do not have a machine stir it vigorously a couple of times while it is freezing to reduce the amount of ice crystals. When it is firm but not hard, pour three-quarters of the ice cream around the base and sides of the mould. Cover well and return to the freezer for a few hours to harden.

When the outer layer is firm prepare the banana ice cream in the same way and pour it inside the mango ice cream layer. Sprinkle the chopped apricot in the centre of the banana ice cream. Spread the remaining mango ice cream over the base. Again cover well and leave overnight to harden.

Remove from the mould half an hour before serving.

Makes 8 portions. Each portion is 25 g CHO. 120 kcals.

Frozen Cherry Cheesecake

Not all cheese cakes come with a base – some consist only of the white cheese filling served in thick slices. This recipe for frozen cheese cake belongs to that category and as well as being superbly creamy it is very quick to make.

225 g (8 oz) low-fat curd cheese
100 g (4 oz) cottage cheese
100 g (4 oz) low-fat fromage frais

150 g (5 oz) peeled banana
400 g (14 oz) black cherries
$\frac{1}{2}$ tsp vanilla essence
few mint leaves, frozen (optional)

Put the cottage cheese through a food mill or sieve to remove the lumps. Combine with the curd cheese and fromage frais. Sieve the banana and stir it into the cheese.

Wash and pat dry the cherries. Slice each cherry into 3 or 4 pieces depending on its size. Stir into the cheese and banana mixture together with the vanilla essence. The mixture will turn a delicate shade of pink.

Pour the cheesecake mixture into a freezer container lined with parchment paper. Cover and freeze for $2\frac{1}{2}$–3 hours until the sides and base are frozen hard and the middle is chilled but still creamy. The length of time this takes depends on how deep your container is and how powerful your freezer. When ready to serve, the cheesecake can be easily removed from the container onto a plate and the parchment paper lifted off. As the cherry pieces are rounded, the cut slices of the cake have an attractive wavy shell pattern. Decorate with frozen mint leaves if desired.

Makes 6 portions. Each portion is 15 g CHO. 100 kcals.

Frozen Fruit

Freeze a punnet of rich red strawberries and pale green seedless grapes and you have a dessert that will delight family and friends. Experiment further with an accompanying fruit sauce or coulis (pages 150–3) and you have created a dinner party dessert.

Fruit for freezing should be bought fresh either the same day from the greengrocer or picked from the garden or from a pick-your-own farm. As well as being fresh, the fruit should not be blemished, bruised or overripe. Freezing diminishes the sweet flavour so choose very sweet fruits such as grapes, melons, mangoes, peaches and bananas. The texture changes during the freezing process so there is more to get your teeth into.

CHILDREN'S PARTIES

Strawberries which have been washed, dried, hulled and speared on a lolly stick and then put in a freezer container until rock-hard are incredibly popular with all children. Even the ones who have been inconsiderate enough to spit out your sugar-free fairy cakes bedecked with pastel coconut icing will come back to ask for more. It is slow work eating strawberry ice lollies so the carbohydrate value remains low, even for those on thirds and fourths. 150 g (5 oz) strawberries are 10 g CHO, 40 kcals.

ADULTS AND CHILDREN

Take 10 frozen seedless *grapes* and 5 frozen *raspberries* per person and serve alongside an Apple and Blackberry Sauce (page 151) to make a luscious dessert.

Bamboo skewers pierced through a selection of fruit can be frozen the day before and whisked out of the freezer ready to serve. A combination of alternating berries and grapes looks very colourful. Use a mixture of raspberries, strawberries, blackberries and seedless green grapes. Another combination is to use slices of banana, peach and mango chunks linked to each other by small green grapes. Both of these versions can be served with an accompanying bowl of fruit coulis for dipping.

Sharon fruit freeze very well. The unreal glow of the orange skin looks supreme when served as a dessert. The fruit can be eaten firm or soft but the skin should not be blemished. It is imported from Israel in the winter months. They taste best when they are no longer frozen solid and it is possible to dig a spoon into the fruit. Remove half an hour to an hour before serving and slice off the top for the lid. They are wonderfully sweet. I would not recommend keeping the sharon fruit in the freezer longer than a couple of days.

The same method can be used for *persimmons* which are imported from Italy in the winter, but they should be really ripe. If not ripe they have a sour astringent taste.

Dessert Cakes

Fancy cakes and gateaux are luxury desserts. Heavy fruit cakes are fine for the tea table but the dessert trolly demands feather-light creations filled with creams or fruit.

Most of the cakes in this section are sweetened with banana. The banana is either puréed through a sieve or food mill, or mashed with a fork and then beaten into egg yolks with an electric whisk. Banana needs subtle handling. If used too generously, everything you bake will taste like banana cake.

The surprising advantage when making a sponge with fruit instead of sugar is that the chances of anything going wrong are dramatically reduced. Harold McGee describes sugar in his book *On Food and Cooking* as a 'structure enfeebling ingredient' in sponges. On discovering that my recipes for sugar-free cakes never flopped, he concluded that the high-fibre content from dried or fresh fruit helped to stabilize the mixture. Bananas contain 3.4 g fibre per 100 grams and dried dates 8.7 g whereas sugar has none at all.

Oven temperature is critical when baking cakes. While recipes specify a cooking temperature, the heat varies with each oven. Older ovens tend to be hotter and have better hot air circulation while new ones require higher settings. While preparing *Sugar-Free Cakes and Biscuits* I had a powerful old gas oven in which I baked all my cakes on gas 4/350°F/180°C. After replacing it with a modern oven I now bake cakes on gas 5/375°F/190°C, on the middle shelf. If you are not happy with the finished result, experiment with your oven temperature and shelf position. Also check that the door closes properly. A sign that the oven is too cool is if the cake does not rise and the inside is not full of air bubbles but rather solid and damp. If the top of the cake burns before the inside is cooked then the oven is too hot or the shelf position is too high. Never let uncooked cake mixture stand around – always pour it immediately into the baking tin and then place in a preheated oven.

These cake recipes use more eggs than those in *Sugar-Free Cakes and Biscuits*, to add the lightness that people expect in a dessert. Current dietary advice is not to eat too many eggs because they are a source of dietary cholesterol. However nutritionists are more concerned these days with blood cholesterol. In an experiment carried out at the Radcliffe Infirmary in Oxford, healthy volunteers ate seven eggs a week, while adjusting the rest of their diet to fibre-rich carbohydrates and greatly reduced saturated fats. Under these conditions the eggs had no effect on blood cholesterol concentration. The study concluded that it was unnecessary to cut back on eggs if people had already limited the amount of saturated fats and increased their fibre intake – the basic proposition underlying the recipes in this book.

All the cakes keep well if you store them in the fridge. I put this to the test when I overcatered for a party. The previous week had been spent piling the freezer high with sponge cakes from this section. It took us five days to finish off all the defrosted cakes, but the last bite still tasted as good as the first. Wrap well in greaseproof paper and silver foil and make sure the cakes do not get wet in the fridge.

Ingredients Used in Dessert Cakes

Wholewheat flour – for best results use the finely milled or pastry flour. It is available in specialist health food shops. If you cannot find any, grind your ordinary flour finely in a food processor as you need it.

Eggs – the size of the eggs used in the cake recipes are large. Buy from a reputable source because of the dangers of salmonella from infected flocks.

Banana – use ripe yellow bananas; the fruit in green-skinned ones is too dry. Either mash well with a fork until smooth or put through a sieve or hand-operated food mill. As before the weight given in recipes is without the peel.

Dates – to make a date paste, simmer the dates with a little water until they can be mashed to a paste with a fork. If a smooth paste is required, blend in a machine.

Sultanas – when used whole, rinse and dry them first. If made into a paste, either mince well in a food processor or simmer with water until the water is absorbed and then blend in a machine. The sultana paste will not be completely smooth.

Carob bars and drops – these are usually made with carob powder, oil, skimmed milk and whey powder, lecithin and sometimes vanilla flavouring. The type most easily available in health food shops in Britain originates from Cyprus. However some brands in health food chains are made with sugar – an unnecessary addition as carob is high in natural sugars. Be sure to read the ingredients' small print before making your purchase.

Carob Vanilla Sponge with Carob Cream

This is a very light moist sponge sandwiched together and decorated on top with a firm carob filling. It is successful as an after-dinner gateau or a fancy tea cake. Even people who are not keen on carob after tasting this cake keep on asking for 'another small slice'. If the quantities are doubled the recipe makes a dramatic four-layered cake.

Carob is made from the pods of trees found in countries around the Mediterranean coast such as Spain, Greece, Lebanon and Israel. The pods are ground to a powder and baked. Unlike cocoa, which is bitter, carob is sweet, containing 46 per cent natural sugar. Another bonus of eating carob is that it is brimming with minerals such as calcium, magnesium, potassium and phosphorus.

Vanilla Sponge
75 g (3 oz) dried dates
150 ml (5 fl oz) water
3 eggs
50 g (2 oz) peeled ripe
   bananas, finely mashed
65 g (2½ oz) fine milled
   wholewheat flour, sieved
¼ tsp bicarbonate of soda
15 g (½ oz) ground almonds
½ tsp vanilla essence

Carob sponge
10 g (½ oz) carob powder
1 tbs low-fat natural yogurt

Carob Cream
100 g (4 oz) carob bar,
   chopped
150 ml (5 fl oz) low-fat fromage frais
desiccated coconut

Grease or oil the bases of two 17 cm (7 inch) diameter baking tins and cover with baking parchment paper. Alternatively grease and line a rectangle tin about 30 × 25 cm (12 × 10 inches) and cut the cake in half when baked. Preheat the oven to gas 6/400°F/200°C.

Heat the dates and water in a small pan until most of the water is absorbed. Mash the dates to a paste with a fork. Leave to cool.

Separate the yolks and whites of the eggs into two bowls. Whisk the egg yolks until pale and creamy. Add the mashed banana and continue whisking until the mixture is fairly smooth. Whisk in the date paste until it is mixed well with the yolk mixture. Stir in the flour, bicarbonate of soda, ground almonds and vanilla essence. Beat the egg whites stiffly and carefully fold them in.

Pour no more than one third of the sponge mixture into a separate bowl. To this add the carob powder mixed with the yogurt. Alternate the vanilla and carob mixture into the lined tins so that swirls of brown nestle next to white. Place immediately in the preheated oven. Bake for 10 minutes, until the cake is browned on top. When the cake is ready turn it out on to a sheet of greaseproof paper.

Prepare the filling: place the chopped carob bar in a bowl in a saucepan of gently bubbling water. Make sure the water does not bubble up over the sides of the bowl. Add the fromage frais as the carob begins to melt. Give an occasional stir with a spoon. As soon as it is thick and creamy spread over the surface of both the cakes. Sandwich together and sprinkle the topping with coconut.

Makes 8 large slices. Each slice is 20 g CHO. 180 kcals.

Carob-Drop Roulade Filled with Ice Cream

This is a dessert of contrasts. A warm sponge roulade spread with creamy ice cream. I tested this on my husband who abhors carob in any form and who can still be found gnawing away at the occasional bar of 80 per cent French chocolate – he pronounced it brilliant.

Read the ingredients carefully on the carob packet to make sure it does not include sugar. If you cannot find drops or buttons use a bar and break it up into small pieces.

3 eggs, separated
125 g (4½ oz) peeled
  banana, sieved
50 g (2 oz) fine milled
  wholewheat flour
25 g (1 oz) ground almonds
½ tsp almond essence

75 g (3 oz) carob drops
2 tbs desiccated coconut
75–100 g (3–4 oz) sugar-free
  plum jam
1 recipe Quick Banana Ice
  Cream (page 91) made in
  advance

Grease or oil the base of a 22.5 × 30 cm (9 × 12 inch) swiss roll tin and place a sheet of greaseproof paper or baking parchment on top. Oil the top surface of the greaseproof paper so that it fits snugly into the corners and sides of the tin. Preheat the oven (gas 6/400°F/200°C).

Whisk the egg yolks until pale. Add the sieved banana and continue to whisk for a little longer until thick and creamy. Whisk the egg whites stiffly and fold these into the egg yolk and banana mixture. Add the fine flour, ground almonds and almond essence and stir in gently with a metal spoon. Fold the carob drops in.

Pour the mixture into the prepared swiss roll tin and spread evenly, making sure you do not skimp near the corners because they will get brown first. Bake for 7–10 minutes in the centre of the oven until the mixture has set and is beginning to turn golden brown. If it becomes too brown it will crack when rolled up.

Have ready prepared a sheet of greaseproof paper the same size as the baking tin and sprinkle it with desiccated coconut. Warm the jam by standing the jar in a bowl of hot water.

Take the swiss roll out of the oven and turn it top side down on to the coconut covered paper. Gently ease the paper off the back of the swiss roll. Spread with the warmed jam and roll up. Wrap the greaseproof paper and a tea towel around the roll to keep it warm.

Remove the ice cream from the freezer one hour before

you want to serve the roulade, to give it time to soften. When ready to serve half open the warm roll and spread the ice cream over the exposed jammy surface. Roll up again and cut into thick slices.

Makes 8 generous portions. Each portion is 25 g CHO. 205 kcals

Carob Hazelnut Cake

'This tastes better then a chocolate cake!' exclaimed one of my panel of tasters. 'I could become seriously addicted to it.'

The feature that I like about this rich cake is that the topping and the cake are made at the same time – the topping is taken off from the cake mixture before it is baked. This is based on a Russian recipe which was handed on to me when I was 16 by an inspired cook whose measurements were handfuls and pinches.

Serve with fromage frais or ice cream. Truly committed carob fans serve it with Hot Carob-Pear Sauce (page 152).

75 g (3 oz) sultanas
75 ml (3 fl oz) water
40 g (1½ oz) margarine
3 tbs freshly squeezed or unsweetened orange juice
100 g (4 oz) carob bar, broken into pieces
2 eggs
50 g (2 oz) ground hazelnuts
125 g (4½ oz) peeled ripe banana
100 g (4 oz) wholewheat flour
1 tsp bicarbonate of soda
100 ml (4 fl oz) low-fat or live yogurt

Rinse the sultanas and put them in a middle-sized heavy saucepan with the water and bring to the boil. Simmer uncovered until most of the water is absorbed. Blend to as fine a paste as possible. Alternatively mince finely in a food processor without first simmering in water.

Return the sultana paste to the saucepan. Add the margarine and orange juice and heat slowly on a low light. As the margarine starts to melt, add the broken up pieces of carob. Once all the margarine has melted, remove from the heat and wait until the rest of the carob melts in the warm liquid. This avoids heating the carob to boiling temperature. Leave to cool for a few minutes.

Separate the eggs. Lightly whisk the egg yolks with a fork and add them a little at a time to the carob mixture. Remove 3 tablespoons of this mixture and put it in the fridge. This is the topping.

Still keeping the mixture in the saucepan stir in the ground hazelnuts. Mash the banana finely and add. Stir in the wholewheat flour, bicarbonate of soda and yogurt. Whisk the egg whites until they are standing in stiff peaks and fold into the cake mixture.

Pour into a 20 cm (8 inch) diameter greased and floured baking tin and bake in a preheated oven (gas 5/375°F/190°C) for 30 minutes. The cake is ready when a knife inserted in the middle comes out cleanly. Remove the cake from the tin and spread the topping over the surface while still warm – it gives a shiny sheen to the cake.

Makes 16 slices. Each slice is 12.5 g CHO. 115 kcals.

Orange-Nut Cake with Orange Sorbet

I created this recipe for Passover, when ground nuts are used instead of flour. The matza meal makes the cake drier than a pudding. Ordinary wholewheat flour could be substituted or coeliacs could use brown rice flour.

The Western Jewish community has a higher than average incidence of diabetes. No one has come forward with a reason why this should be so. However research has shown that where a community eats hardly any sugar diabetes is virtually unknown. This was the case with the Yemenite Jewish community. After they moved to Israel in the early fifties and largely ate the typical high-sugar, high-fat Western diet for a number of years they had the same figures for diabetes and heart disease as the rest of the population.

225 g (8 oz) peeled ripe banana
50 g (2 oz) raisins
3 eggs
zest of ½ orange (use organic if possible)

125 g (4½ oz) ground hazelnuts
50 g (2 oz) ground almonds
15 g (½ oz) fine matza meal
1 recipe Orange Sorbet (page 106)

Mash the banana finely so it becomes liquid. Wash and dry the raisins, and chop them.

Separate the eggs. Whisk the egg yolks until they are creamy. Add the mashed banana and continue to whisk until the mixture is smooth.

Stir in the chopped raisins, orange zest, ground nuts and matza meal (or substitutes).

Whisk the egg whites stiffly and fold them into the mixture. Pour into a greased 20 cm (8 inch) diameter baking tin lined with baking parchment paper. Bake in the middle of a preheated oven (gas 5/375°F/190°C) for 30–40 minutes, until the cake is evenly browned on top and a knife inserted in the middle comes out cleanly. Leave to cool and remove from the tin. Store in a cool place.

Follow the instructions to prepare the sorbet and serve with slices of the cake.

Makes 12 slices. Each slice is 7.5 g CHO. 95 kcals. Each slice served with orange sorbet is 15 g CHO. 125 kcals.

Cheesecake with Velvet Carob Topping

This recipe is a revision of one that first appeared in *Sugar-Free Cakes and Biscuits*. This version is sweeter and creamier. The first version was always popular but this one walks straight off the table.

Smatana is made from skimmed milk and cream and contains 10 per cent fat. If you cannot find it in your local shop combine equal amounts of yogurt and sour cream.

Crust
15 g (½ oz generous) dried
   dates
50 ml (2 fl oz) water
50 ml (2 fl oz) skimmed
   milk
15 g (½ oz) carob powder
40 g (1½ oz) Shredded
   Wheat

Filling
2 eggs, separated
125 g (4½ oz) peeled
   banana,
finely mashed
250 g (9 oz) low-fat curd
   cheese
50 g (2 oz) raisins
1 tbs freshly squeezed
   lemon juice
25 g (1 oz) ground
   almonds

Topping
125 ml (4½ fl oz) smatana
20 g (3/4 oz) carob powder
½ tsp vanilla essence
2 tbs orange juice

For the crust, heat the dates with the water in a small pan until most of the water is absorbed and the dates can be mashed with a fork. Add the milk and carob and stir until a thick paste is formed. Remove from the heat. Crumble the Shredded Wheat into the carob mixture and stir until well coated and dark brown. Pat the mixture evenly over the base of a 20 cm (8 inch) diameter baking dish. There is no need to grease the dish as the crust softens with the cheese mixture on top and can easily be served from the baking dish.

Prepare the filling: whisk the egg yolks until pale. Whisk in the finely mashed banana (or sieve first if not using an electric whisk) until it has a smooth, creamy consistency. Fold in the curd cheese, raisins, ground almonds and lemon juice. Whisk the egg whites into stiff peaks and fold into the cheese mixture. Pour this evenly over the crust. Bake in a preheated oven (gas 4/350°F/180°C) for 20–25 minutes, until the cake is set and firm at the edges. It should not be very runny in the middle – if it is, let it cook a little longer. (If doubling the quantity of the recipe, cook it about 10–15 minutes longer so that the middle is virtually set).

Remove the cheese cake from the oven and pour the combined topping ingredients – smatana, carob powder, vanilla and orange juice evenly over the surface. Return to the oven for a further 5 minutes. Cool. Store in the fridge for up to three days.

Makes 12 slices. Each slice is 10 g CHO. 80 kcals

Ricotta Cheesecake

Ricotta cheese is an Italian curd cheese that is sold in blocks and contains 11 g fat per 100 grams – about the same amount of fat as Greek yogurt.

1 recipe Sweet Shortcrust
   Pastry (page 22)
ground cinnamon

Filling
200 g (7 oz) fresh dates

3 eggs, separated
100 g (4 oz) peeled banana,
   mashed
400 g (14 oz) ricotta cheese
1 tsp lemon zest

Roll out three quarters of the pastry to cover a rectangular 20 × 25 cm (8 × 10 inch) baking dish or 22.5 cm (9 inch) diameter dish about 3.5 cm (1½ inch) deep. Bake in a moderate preheated oven (gas 4/350°F/180°C) until it is a light biscuit colour and just beginning to brown on the sides.

Wash the dates, remove the stones and chop into 1 cm (½ inch) pieces. Whisk the egg yolks until creamy and pale. Add the mashed banana and whisk with an electric whisk until it is a fairly smooth consistency. (If working with a hand whisk sieve the banana first). Mash the ricotta and fold in with the lemon zest and chopped dates. Whisk the egg whites and stir in.

Pour the filling into the pastry case. Roll out the remaining pastry about the same thickness as the base and cut into strips. As it is a short pastry, and can be difficult to handle, an alternative method is to make pieces of pastry into balls and roll them between your hands into long strips. Flatten these with a rolling pin. Cut into strips and make into a loose lattice over the surface of the cheese filling, meeting the sides of the pastry case. Cut any remaining pastry into small star shapes and place at strategic positions over a strip. Sprinkle the stars lightly with cinnamon.

Bake in a preheated oven (gas 4/350°F/180°C) for 30–40 minutes, until set firm and the pastry strips are browned. Test the cake with a knife – when it comes out cleanly the cake is ready. Leave to cool.

Makes 12 slices. Each slice is 20 g CHO. 205 kcals.

Fruit-Spice Cake

The fun of this cake is that the creamy fruit filling is baked with the cake. Store it in a cool place or the fridge.

150 g (5 oz) dried dates
300 ml (11 fl oz) water
150 g (5 oz) wholewheat
  flour
25 g (1 oz) soya flour
50 g (2 oz) ground almonds
1½–2 tsp mixed spice
1½–2 tsp ground cinnamon
1 tsp bicarbonate of soda
2 tsp cream of tartar
75 ml (3 fl oz) oil
3 eggs
150 ml (5 fl oz) low-fat
  natural yogurt

Filling
200 g (7 oz) peeled banana
100 ml (4 fl oz) low-fat
  natural yogurt
100 g (4 oz) ripe cherries,
  chopped
50 g (2 oz) mango, peeled
  and chopped
1 egg

Cherry coulis (optional)
200 g (7 oz) cherries
2 tbs unsweetened apple
  juice

Cook the dates in the water on a low heat until all the water has been absorbed by the dates and a thick paste has formed. Blend to make it really smooth. Cool.

Prepare the chopped fruit for the filling and put to one side.

Mix together the wholewheat and soya flour, ground almonds, spices, bicarbonate of soda and cream of tartar. Stir in the oil and date paste. Whisk the eggs well – beating a lot of air into the eggs helps to make the cake light. Fold in the eggs then add the yogurt to give a mixture with a thick pouring consistency.

Pour half the mixture into a deep greased and floured 20 cm (8 inch) diamter tin.

Prepare the filling: mash the banana finely with a fork. Combine it with the yogurt. Add the chopped cherries and mango. Whisk the egg and mix with the other ingredients.

Pour the filling over the cake mixture in the baking tin. It spreads easily as it has a more liquid consistency.

Spoon the remaining cake mixture over the filling. Make

sure all the fruit is covered. Smooth the surface with the back of a spoon.

Bake in a preheated oven (gas 4/350°F/170°C) for 40–45 minutes. Test by putting a knife in the middle of the cake and checking to see it comes out cleanly.

Serve either with a thin layer of fromage frais spread over the top or with a cherry coulis made by stoning the cherries and blending with the apple juice.

Makes 12 slices. Each slice with either fromage frais or cherry coulis is 25 g CHO. 220 kcals.

Blueberry Squares

It is only in the last few years that it has been possible to find that great American dream – blueberries – in supermarkets and specialist greengrocers. American friends assure me that what we buy here is a poor cousin of the fresh version found across the Ocean but the taste is different enough to make it worth using.

This dessert can be prepared either on the day it is to be served or the sponge base can be prepared the day before and only the fruit topping left for the following day.

Sponge base
75 g (3 oz) dried dates
150 ml (5 fl oz) water
50 g (2 oz) peeled banana
3 eggs
65 g (2½ oz generous) fine milled wholewheat flour
½ tsp almond essence

Blueberry topping
300 g (11 oz) blueberries
100 ml (4 fl oz) unsweetened apple juice
2 tsp freshly squeezed lemon juice
1 heaped tsp arrowroot

Cover a rectangular baking tin about 25 × 30 cm (10 × 12

inches) with greased baking parchment paper. Preheat the oven (gas 6/400°F/200°C).

Heat the dates and water in a small pan until the water is almost absorbed. Mash to a paste with a fork and leave to cool. Mash the banana finely. Separate the eggs. Whisk the egg yolks until pale and creamy. Add the banana and continue whisking until it becomes a thick smooth liquid, then whisk in the date paste. Stir in the flour and almond essence. Whisk the egg whites until they form stiff peaks and fold in with a metal spoon. Pour into the prepared tin and bake for 7–10 minutes until it turns a light golden brown and is firm to the touch. Turn out onto a wire tray to cool. When cool cut into 12 equal squares.

For the topping, pour the apple and lemon juice into a stainless steel saucepan. Take off 1 dessertspoon of the liquid to dissolve the arrowroot in and then pour back into the pan. Add the blueberries and bring to the boil. After about 10 seconds the juice becomes purple. Take off the heat and remove the blueberries with a slotted spoon. Boil the remaining liquid a little longer until it thickens. Pour the liquid over the blueberries and leave until cool.

To assemble: spoon the blueberries and liquid over the sponge squares – the sponge squares become streaked with the purple juice. Leave in a cool place until ready to serve.

Makes 12 squares. Each square is 10 g CHO. 80 kcals.

Carrot Cake with Sultana Cream

Carotene, a valuable source of vitamin A, lives in greatest concentration in, you have probably guessed, carrots. If you want a carotene boost, there are up to 14,000 micrograms of it in every 100 grams of carrots – more in older carrots than young ones. Deficiency of vitamin A can lead to eye damage – an early warning sign is difficulty with seeing at night. Hence the popular notion that carrots improve night vision.

I tend to buy organic carrots, because they taste better and are pesticide free. *Food Magazine* reported that government monitoring had revealed that one out of every three carrots contains triazophos, a pesticide, at higher levels than recommended. Apparently the Ministry of Agriculture proposed solving this by raising the recommended levels. Whatever you make of this conflicting approach to figures, the best test is to taste organic carrots yourself.

2 eggs, separated
100 g (4 oz) peeled banana, mashed
75 g (3 oz) dried dates
150 ml (5 fl oz) water
150 g (5 oz) carrot, finely grated
100 g (4 oz) wholewheat flour
1 tsp cream of tartar
½ tsp bicarbonate of soda
1 level tsp mixed spice
1 tsp ground cardamom

1 tbs lemon juice
zest of half a lemon (organic if possible)
40 g (1½ oz) raw pistachio nuts, coarsely chopped

To decorate
1 recipe Sultana Cream (page 70)
desiccated coconut
25 g (1 oz) sugar-free apricot jam

Whisk the egg yolks well. Add the mashed bananas and continue to whisk until the mixture is pale and smooth.

Make a paste with the dates and water, cooking them over a low heat until the water has been absorbed and the dates can be mashed into a paste with a fork. Stir in with the grated carrot.

To the egg yolkes and bananas, add the flour, cream of tartar, bicarbonate of soda, mixed spice, cardamom, lemon juice and zest, pistachios and carrot and date paste.

Whisk the egg whites until they become stiff white peaks.

Fold them in and pour the mixture into a greased and floured 20 cm (8 inch) diameter cake tin. Bake in a pre-heated oven (gas 5/375°F/190°C) for 30–35 minutes. The cake will be browned on top and firm to the touch.

Decorate with desiccated coconut sprinkled over a thin layer of sugar-free jam and pipe decorative flourishes with the sultana cream.

Makes 16 slices. Each slice is 10 g CHO. 65 kcals. Each slice with sultana cream is 10 g CHO. 75 kcals.

Semolina Cake with Orange Sauce

3 large eggs
175 g (6 oz) peeled banana, finely mashed
175 g (6 oz) fresh dates (weighed with stones), stoned and chopped
1 lemon, grated (use organic if possible)
juice of half a lemon

100 g (4 oz) wholegrain semolina
25 g (1 oz) wholewheat flour
25 g (1 oz) flaked almonds

1 recipe Orange Sauce (page 152)

Separate the eggs. Whisk the egg yolks well until they are pale yellow. Add the banana and continue to whisk with an electric whisk until you obtain a fairly smooth consistency. If using a hand whisk, sieve the banana first. Stir in the chopped dates, lemon zest and juice, flour and sieved semolina. Whisk the egg whites until they are standing in stiff peaks. Fold them gently into the rest of the cake mixture.

Grease a 25 × 20 cm (10 × 8 inch) baking tin, cover with baking parchment paper and pour the cake mixture in, making sure that the surface is even. Cover the surface with the flaked almonds. Place in a preheated oven (gas 4/350°F/

180°C) for about 30 minutes, until it is a golden brown colour and a knife comes out cleanly from the centre. Serve with the orange sauce.

Makes 12 slices. Each slice is 10 g CHO. 85 kcals. Each slice with orange sauce is 15 g CHO. 95 kcals.

Birthday Fruit Layer

This cake was made for my husband's birthday. He does not like creams of any description so I made this multi-layered fruit slice sponge which looks special and can be prepared the day before.

Sponge
75 g (3 oz) dried dates
150 ml (5 fl oz) water
3 eggs
50 g (2 oz) peeled ripe
   banana
65 g (2½ oz) fine milled
   wholewheat flour, sieved
25 g (1 oz) ground almonds
½ tsp almond essence

Fillings
300 g (11 oz) strawberries
150 g (5 oz) black cherries
150–175 g (5–6 oz) large
   seedless green grapes
100 g (4 oz) sugar-free
   plum jam
1 tsp lemon juice
unsweetened desiccated
   coconut

Grease or oil the base of two 25 × 30 cm (10 × 12 inch) tins and place a sheet of baking parchment on top.

Put the dried dates and water in a small pan and simmer until most of the water has been absorbed. Mash to a paste with a fork. Leave to cool.

Separate the eggs. Whisk the egg yolks until they are pale and creamy. Mash the banana to a liquid purée and whisk well with the egg yolks, then whisk in the cooled date paste until it is thoroughly incoporated. Stir in the flour, ground almonds and almond essence. Whisk the egg whites until they stand in stiff peaks and fold these in gently.

Spread the sponge mixture thinly and equally over the surface of the two tins. Bake in a preheated oven (gas 6/ 400°F/200°C) for 7–10 minutes, until the sponge is just beginning to turn brown. Remove from the oven and invert on to a sheet of greaseproof paper to cool.

Cut each of the sponges in half so that there are now four layers waiting to be filled.

Prepare the fruit: wash, hull and pat dry the strawberries. Slice thinly and divide in half between two bowls. Wash and pat dry the cherries. Cut them in half, removing the stones. Wash and pat dry the grapes and cut in half lengthways.

Spread the first layer of sponge with a little of the jam. The purpose of the jam is not so much to sweeten as to make sure that the fruit sticks to the sponge base. Cover with one of the bowls of sliced strawberries. It is important to keep the fruit layers even otherwise the sponge layer on top will be bumpy.

Place a second sponge layer on top. Again, spread thinly with jam and lay the cherry halves across the surface. Cover with the third sponge layer. Spread thinly with jam and lay the last bowl of sliced strawberries on top. Cover with the final sponge layer. Spread thinly with jam and carefully lay out the grapes over the entire surface.

Spoon the remaining jam into a small saucepan with the teaspoon of lemon juice and heat for a few seconds until it dissolves. Spread over the surface of the grapes and then sprinkle them with a little desiccated coconut.

Wrap the cake well with baking parchment paper, so that it is sealed all the way round, and leave to stand in the fridge overnight.

Makes 12 slices of fruit layer cake. Each slice is 15 g CHO. 105 kcals.

Yeast Cakes

These are typical Central European cakes. The basic concept of the cakes is to combine a rich bread dough with dried or fresh fruit.

The yeast pastry uses vitamin C (ascorbic acid), which makes it rise more quickly than sugar and also removes one of the proving stages in the traditional approach. The nutritional benefit of using yeast in pastry is that the leavening process helps the breakdown of phytates found in wheat fibre. Phytates can limit the absorption of minerals such as calcium, iron and zinc by the body. If your diet is made up of yeast-based bread with occasional high-fibre biscuits or cakes this will not have a dramatic effect, but if you suffer from a deficiency of these minerals you should avoid unleavened bread and bran-based foods until the shortage has been made up.

If you cannot find a 25 mg tablet of vitamin C buy the 50 mg size and cut it in half.

Yeast Pastry

400 g (14 oz) finely milled wholewheat flour
25 g (1 oz) fresh yeast
25 mg tablet of vitamin C
200 ml (7 fl oz) water
60 g (2 oz generous) margarine

1 egg, lightly whisked
100 g (4 oz) peeled banana, puréed
2 tsp vanilla essence

Pour the flour into a large mixing bowl. Crumble the yeast

and crush the vitamin C tablet into a small bowl. Heat the water until it is lukewarm and pour a little over the yeast and vitamin C to make a creamy mixture. Melt the fat in the rest of the water. Add these two liquids to the flour. Stir in the lightly whisked egg, puréed banana and vanilla. Work the mixture into a dough with your hands and turn on to a lightly floured board or worktop and knead for about 5 minutes, or for about 1 minute in a food processor. Return to the bowl and cover the top with a clean tea towel and leave to rest for 10 minutes in a warm room. The pastry is then ready to be rolled out.

Yeast pastry is 280 g CHO. 1875 kcals.

Prune Roll

A light yeast pastry interlaced with softened prunes and decorated with coconut icing. Serve as it is or with low-fat fromage frais.

½ recipe Yeast Pastry
(page 139)

Filling
250 g (9 oz) pitted prunes
300 ml (11 fl oz) water
100 g (4 oz) ground
almonds
4 tsps mixed spice

50 ml (2 fl oz) freshly
squeezed or unsweet-
ened orange juice

Icing (optional)
50 g (2 oz) coconut cream,
chopped
150 ml (5 fl oz) water
flaked almonds

Prepare the filling: simmer the prunes in the water until they are softened and the water is absorbed. Pour on to a shallow plate and leave to cool – any extra liquid tends to be absorbed while standing. Mix the ground almonds, spice and juice together to make a crumbly paste.

Roll out the pastry thinly on a floured board into a rectangle about 45 × 30 cm (18 × 12 inches). Sprinkle the almond paste over the surface of the pastry. Lay the prunes over the top, with even spaces between them. Roll the pastry up tightly and seal the ends. Place it on a greased baking tray, bending it into a 'U' shape. Cover with a tea towel and leave to stand in a warm room for 20 minutes while the pastry expands. Bake in a preheated oven (gas 5/ 375°F/190°C) for 30–35 minutes, until the pastry is browned and the surface sounds hollow if you tap it.

To make the icing: heat the cut-up coconut cream and water in a medium-sized saucepan until the pieces of coconut cream have dissolved, forming a thickish white paste. Spread along the top of the baked prune roll. Decorate with a few flaked almonds that have been browned under the grill.

Makes 12 slices. Each slice is 20 g CHO. 175 kcals.

Apple-Pear Yeast Cake

This cake is made in a ring mould which guarantees that it will look very impressive. It can be decorated with a strip of carob icing along the top or left as it is – both versions are supremely mouthwatering. The cake keeps well for three days if stored in a cool place.

½ recipe Yeast Pastry
  (page 139)

Filling
675 g (1 lb 8 oz) eating
  apples
325 g (11½ oz) firm pears

3–4 tsps ground cinnamon

Carob icing
25 g (1 oz) carob bar,
  broken in pieces
50 ml (2 fl oz) live yogurt
15 g (½ oz) flaked almonds

Prepare the filling: grate the apples and pears and mix with the cinnamon.

Roll out the pastry so that there is enough to fill a 22.5 cm (9 inch) diameter greased ring mould around the base and sides with enough left over for the top. When you have lined the ring mould with the pastry, pack in the grated fruit. Cover with pastry over the top, pinching the inner and outer sides together. If there is any left-over pastry, roll it into a thin strip and use it to reinforce the joins.

Cover the ring with a tea towel and leave to stand in a warm room for 20 minutes, until the pastry has expanded. Bake in a preheated oven (gas 5/375°F/190°C) for 30–35 minutes, until well browned on top.

Insert a knife carefully around the inner and outer sides and invert the tin on to a plate to remove the cake from the mould.

Prepare the icing: melt the carob in a bowl over gently bubbling water. Stir in the yogurt and let them melt together. Spread over the top of the cake and decorate with the flaked almonds.

Makes 12 large slices. Each slice is 20 g CHO. 125 kcals.

Nibbles

Carrot Halva

My neighbour, Nili Patel, is a superb cook and always giving me dishes to sample from her kitchen. She worked with me on this recipe for a sugar-free, virtually fat-free halva. The method we devised is simple but it does take time. If you have never seen a vegetable halva before, go window-shopping at any Indian sweet shop.

350 g (12 oz) carrot
125 g (4½ oz) dried dates
300 ml (11 fl oz) skimmed milk

10 g (½ oz) ghee or butter
1½–2 tsp ground cardamom

Peel the carrot and grate finely. Grind the dates. (They can be cooked with a little water and mashed if grinding is not possible but the carrot mixture will need to be cooked longer to ensure the extra moisture is absorbed.)

Heat the 300 ml milk in a thick-based pan, add the carrots and boil until the milk appears to be absorbed, stirring from time to time for about 10 minutes.

Add the ghee or butter so that the carrot does not burn and continue to cook over a lower heat, stirring every few minutes. Continue to do this for about 5 minutes.

Add the cardamom and continue to cook slowly for 5 minutes. Stir in the ground dates and cook for 20 minutes more, until all the liquid is absorbed. Test it by squeezing the grated carrot between your fingers to make sure no liquid is left. It should form a mass sticking together.

Grease a 20 cm (8 inch) diameter baking dish and pour the halva into it, spreading it over the surface and patting down evenly. Allow to cool for at least 30 minutes. Cut into small shapes when ready to serve. The taste is so rich you can only eat a little at a time.

Makes 24 portions. Each portion is 5 g CHO. 25 kcals.

Carob-Clementine Slices

350 g (12 oz) seedless   100 g (4 oz) carob bar
   clementines

Peel 200 g (7 oz) of the clementines. Remove the pith and divide into segments.

Break the carob bar into small pieces and place in a bowl in a shallow pan filled with boiling water. Leave until it has melted. Be very careful that no water gets into the bowl. As soon as the carob has melted, dip the segments into the bowl, still standing in the hot water, and coat as much of them as possible. Leave to harden on a sheet of greaseproof paper or a marble slab.

Cover well and store for a few hours until needed. Peel and segment the remaining clementines and arrange them on a plate with the coated segments of clementine.

Total amount of CHO is 60 g. 650 kcals.

Carob-Fig Slices

This is the kind of sweet that you keep on nibbling.

200 g (7 oz) dried figs
200 g (7 oz) ground
  almonds
150 g (5 oz) peeled banana,
  mashed
½ tsp lemon zest

50 g (2 oz) carob powder
½ tsp ground cinnamon
2 egg whites
30 g (1 oz) sugar-free jam
unsweetened desiccated
  coconut

Grind the figs in the small bowl of a food processor and mix with the ground almonds and banana. Add the lemon zest, carob powder and cinnamon. Whisk the egg whites until they are standing in peaks and stir in.

Grease a 20 × 25 cm (8 × 10 inch) diameter baking dish and spread the mixture over the base. Even the surface with the back of a spoon. Bake in a preheated oven (gas 3/325°F/170°C) for 35–45 minutes until it is set firm.

Remove from the oven and spread thinly with jam and sprinkle all over the surface with coconut. Cut into 32 pieces.

Makes 32 slices. Each slice is 5 g CHO. 60 kcals.

Date Sweetmeat

A sweet-tasting delight to serve with a hot drink.

200 g (7 oz) fresh dates
⅛ tsp cardamom

100 g (4 oz) walnuts, finely
  chopped

Wash the dates and remove the stones.

Chop the dates finely and mash with the walnuts and the spice. If using a food processor only, use it in bursts otherwise the consistency will be like a purée rather than textured. Divide the paste into 8 balls and place in paper cases to serve. Store in the fridge until needed.

Makes 8 sweetmeats. Each one is 7.5 g CHO. 100 kcals.

Stuffed Prunes

Prunes are recommended by the medical profession for their mild laxative action. But this pragmatic approach overlooks the fact that they have an extremely pleasing taste and across the Channel gourmets get quite excited about them. French towns such as Agen, Marmande, Metz and Tours are famous for the particular variety of prune they produce. The other virtue of prunes is that they are a source of minerals such as calcium, magnesium and iron.

200 g (7 oz) pitted prunes (about 24)
250 ml (9 fl oz) water

Filling
25 g (1 oz) dried dates
50 g (2 oz) almond flakes
50 g (2 oz) chopped pistachios

Cook the prunes in the water in a covered saucepan for about 10 minutes until they are soft but not falling apart. Remove from the pan with a slotted spoon.

For the filling, chop the dates and simmer in the prunes' cooking water until they can be mashed with a fork and the liquid has been absorbed. Brown the almond flakes under the grill or in the oven and put them in a bowl with the pistachio nuts. Bind with the date paste. Cool. The consistency should not be too liquid. Slit open one side of the prunes and fill generously with the nut mixture. Store in the fridge until ready to serve.

Makes 24 stuffed prunes. Each prune is 5 g CHO. 40 kcals.

Stuffed Dates

These come under the category of minimal effort, maximum effect. But this is not the only reason to include them
in your repertoire – they are a favourite with adults and
children.

Make the stuffed dates in early autumn when the first of
the new crop arrives in the greengrocers' and the last of the
summer strawberries are still available. Avoid using strawberries grown out of season because although the colour is
right, the taste never is.

250 g (9 oz) fresh dates   12 plump strawberries
   (about 12)   (weighing about 150 g/5
                                      oz)

Wash and dry the dates. Cut open along one side and
remove the stone. Wash, hull and pat the strawberries dry.
Place them whole in the centre of the dates. Serve immediately or store in the fridge until needed later the same day.

Makes 12 stuffed dates. 2 are 12.5 g CHO. 50 kcals.

Cinnamon Sticks

75 g (3 oz) ground hazel-   60 g (2 oz generous) dried
   nuts   dates
50 g (2 oz) ground almonds   100 ml (4 fl oz) water
1 tsp ground cinnamon   2 tbs rosewater
¼ tsp ground cardamom   1 egg white, stiffly beaten

Combine the hazelnuts, almonds and spices in a bowl. Put
the dates, water and rosewater in a small saucepan and

simmer on a low heat until the water has been absorbed. Mash with a fork to make a paste. Stir the date paste into the ground nuts. Fold in the beaten egg white to make a moist paste.

Divide into 12 pieces and roll each piece into a stick about 7.5 cm (3 inches) long. Bake on a lightly greased tray in a preheated oven (gas 3/325°F/170°C) for 25–30 minutes, until lightly browned on the outside.

Makes 12 sticks. 2 sticks are 7.5 g CHO. 120 kcals.

Almond Thins

These delicate biscuits can be served with fruit fools or ice cream. They are crisp around the edges and soft in the middle.

50 g (2 oz) margarine or
  butter
50 g (2 oz) dried dates,
  chopped finely
50 g (2 oz) wholewheat
  flour

50 g (2 oz) ground almonds
2 tbs freshly squeezed
  orange juice
few drops of almond
  essence

Melt the margarine in a small saucepan and add the chopped dates, stirring with the back of a large spoon so that the dates are squashed and well softened. Add the flour, ground almonds and orange juice and continue stirring over a low light until the mixture comes together in a ball. Remove from the heat and add the almond essence. Drop teaspoons of the mixture on a greased baking tray, flattening them with the back of a spoon so that they are quite thin. The mixture should make 20 flat oval shapes.

Bake in a preheated oven (gas mark 3/325°F/170°C) for 20–25 minutes until the biscuits are just turning brown at the edges. Remove with a palette knife and leave to cool on a wire tray. They can be prepared the day before and stored in a tin.

Makes 20 biscuits. 3 biscuits are 10 g CHO. 140 kcals.

Fruit Sauces

A finishing touch to a special dessert, a fruit sauce transforms a plain cake or fritter into a restaurant treat.

Apple Sauce

550 g (1 lb 4 oz) eating   ½ tsp ground cinnamon
   apples

Wash and slice the apples and simmer in 4 tbs water with the cinnamon until softened. Add more water if necessary to stop the apples catching on the pan. Blend. Serve warm or cold.

Sauce is 50 g CHO. 190 kcals.

Melba Sauce

Dame Nellie Melba, the Australian soprano, took her stage name from her native city of Melbourne. Many dishes were named after her, including this sauce. One of the other famous ones is Peach Melba: 'The chef of the Savoy Hotel in London, the renowned Escoffier, was desolate at being unable to get tickets for her sold-out gala performance. Melba somehow obtained him two seats. Next day at lunch, an extraordinary dessert made its debut at her table accompanied by a note from the chef, saying he had named it after her: *Peach Melba.*' (Norman Lebrecht, *The Book of Musical Anecdotes*).

This is a seasonal sauce that uses raspberries and nectarine. It can be frozen for later in the year. The quantity given is enough for six generous servings with ice cream or a fruit dessert.

350 g (12 oz) fresh raspberries

2 ripe nectarines weighing about 225 g (8 oz)

100 ml (4 fl oz) unsweetened apple juice

Use a blender to convert quickly the raspberries, sliced nectarine and juice to a purée. Alternatively put the raspberries and nectarine through a hand food mill. Sieve the fruit purée to remove the raspberry seeds. Pour into a medium saucepan and bring to the boil for about 15 seconds. The sauce can then be served either hot or cold.

Sauce is 55 g CHO. 235 kcals.

Apple and Blackberry Sauce

200 g (7 oz) blackberries

100 ml (4 fl oz) unsweetened apple juice

250 g (9 oz) eating apple

150 ml (5 fl oz) low-fat natural yogurt or live yogurt

Blend the blackberries and apple juice in the liquidizer. Slice the apple and add with the yogurt and blend again. Sieve and chill in the fridge until needed.

Sauce is 60 g CHO. 270 kcals.

Pink Sauce

2 oranges weighing about
   150 g (5 oz) each

300 g (11 oz) fresh strawberries, washed and
   hulled

Peel the oranges and remove all the pith and pips. Put the segments in a blender or food processor together with the strawberries to make a fruit purée. Sieve this into a saucepan and bring to the boil, then remove from the heat. Serve warm or cold.

Sauce is 40 g CHO. 160 kcals.

Hot Carob-Pear Sauce

600 g (1 lb 5 oz) ripe pears
1½ tbs unsweetened apple
   juice

75 g (3 oz) carob bar

Wash the skin of the pears, cut away any blemished skin, chop and blend in a liquidizer with the apple juice to make a thick smooth liquid. Pour this into a medium-sized pan and slowly heat. Break up the carob bar into the pan and stir with a wooden spoon while it slowly melts.

This is a very thick sauce and is most delicious served hot.

Sauce is 80 g CHO. 600 kcals.

Orange Sauce

200 ml (7 fl oz) unsweet-
   ened orange juice, or
   the juice of 2 oranges

1½–2 tsp arrowroot

Combine the arrowroot with a little of the liquid to make a smooth paste. Add the rest of the liquid and heat over a low light until it comes to the boil and thickens. Allow to simmer for a few minutes, stirring all the time. Serve warm.

Sauce is 20 g CHO. 80 kcals.

Cherry Coulis

200 g (7 oz) cherries   2 tbs unsweetened apple juice

Wash and stone the cherries and blend with the apple juice. Serve chilled.

Sauce is 25 g CHO. 95 kcals.

Quick Peach Cream Sauce

A speedy recipe for those occasions when the fruit cupboard is empty and all you have is some tinned fruit in natural juice. This recipe specifies peaches but you can use any type of tinned fruit. Pour all the fruit and juice into the liquidizer and add a quarter of its weight in yogurt or fromage frais and blend. The result is a luscious cream which can be spooned over puddings, tarts and fritters.

1 tin peaches in natural   100 g (4 oz) low-fat yogurt
   juice weighing 400 g   or Greek yogurt or
   (14 oz)   fromage frais

Blend all the ingredients together and serve.

Sauce is 40 g CHO. 190–270 kcals (depending on type of yogurt used)

Food Values

Food	Amount	CHO approx	Calories approx	Fibre approx
	(neg = negligible; n/a = information not available)			
Almonds, shelled	25 g (1 oz)	neg	140	3.6 g
Apple, eating, medium	110 g (4 oz)	10 g	40	1.7 g
Apple flakes	25 g (1 oz)	23 g	90	n/a
Apple juice, unsweetened	150 ml (5 fl oz)	18 g	70	neg
Apricots, dried raw	25 g (1 oz)	10 g	45	6.0 g
Apricots, fresh	160 g (5½ oz)	10 g	40	3.0 g
Arrowroot	25 g (1 oz)	24 g	90	n/a
Banana, peeled	50 g (2 oz)	10 g	40	1.7 g
Barley, raw	25 g (1 oz)	18 g	85	0.9 g
Barley flour	25 g (1 oz)	19 g	90	0.6 g
Beans, aduki, raw	25 g (1 oz)	10 g	70	6.3 g
Blackberries, raw	160 g (5½ oz)	10 g	45	11.7 g
Blueberries	150 g (5 oz)	10 g	45	3.6 g
Bran, wheat	25 g (1 oz)	5 g	45	11.0 g
Brandy	15 ml (½ fl oz)	neg	35	neg
Cape Gooseberries	100 g (4 oz)	11 g	53	n/a
Carob bar or drops (sugar-free)	25 g (1 oz)	10 g	138	1.7 g
Carob powder	25 g (1 oz)	12 g	50	13.8 g
Carrot, raw	100 g (4 oz)	11 g	45	5.8 g
Carrot juice	25 ml (1 fl oz)	n/a	n/a	neg
Cherries, fresh whole	100 g (4 oz)	10 g	40	1.5 g

Chestnuts, dried	25 g (1 oz)	22 g	105	n/a
Chestnuts, fresh, skinned	25 g (1 oz)	10 g	45	1.7 g
Clementines	115 g (4 oz)	10 g	45	1.7 g
Coconut cream	25 g (1 oz)	neg	160	n/a
Coconut milk	200 g (7 oz)	10 g	40	n/a
Coconut, desiccated	25 g (1 oz)	neg	150	5.9 g
Corn (maize) meal	15 g (½ oz)	11 g	55	0.3 g
Cottage cheese	25 g (1 oz)	neg	25	neg
Custard squash	250 g (9 oz)	10 g	38	n/a
Dates, dried without stones	15 g (½ oz)	10 g	30	1.1 g
Dates, fresh	50 g (2 oz)	10 g	40	n/a
Egg, size 3	1	neg	75	neg
Figs, dried raw	20 g (⅔ oz)	10 g	40	3.7 g
Flour, brown rice	25 g (1 oz)	20 g	90	n/a
Flour, soya, low-fat	35 g (1⅓ oz)	10 g	125	5.0 g
Flour, wholewheat	15 g (½ oz)	10 g	50	1.4 g
Fromage frais	100 g (4 oz)	3 g	45	neg
Gooseberries, cooking	335 g (11½ oz)	10 g	64	9.7 g
Grapes, black, whole	75 g (3 oz)	10 g	40	0.2 g
Hazelnuts, shelled	25 g (1 oz)	2 g	95	1.5 g
Jam, sugar-free	25 g (1 oz)	9 g	30	n/a
Kombu	25 g (1 oz)	n/a	n/a	n/a
Kumquats	100 g (4 oz)	9 g	43	3.8 g
Lemon	100 g (4 oz)	1 g	9	n/a
Lime	100 g (4 oz)	1 g	6	n/a
Lychees	110 g (4 oz)	10 g	40	1.0 g
Mango, raw, flesh only	65 g (2½ oz)	10 g	40	1.0 g
Matza meal	15 g (½ oz)	12 g	52	0.6 g
Margarine, polyunsaturated	25 g (1 oz)	neg	185	neg

Marmalade, sugar-free	25 g (1 oz)	9 g	30	n/a
Melon, galia, flesh only	200 g (7 oz)	10 g	40	1.8 g
Melon, yellow weighed with rind	320 g (11½ oz)	10 g	40	1.9 g
Milk, skimmed	200 ml (7 fl oz)	10 g	65	neg
Millet flakes	15 g (½ oz)	11 g	55	0.7 g
Nectarine	100 g (4 oz)	12 g	50	2.4 g
Oats, porridge	15 g (½ oz)	11 g	60	1.1 g
Oat bran (with germ)	25 g (1 oz)	15 g	105	3.5 g
Oil (sunflower, soya bean, vegetable)	15 ml (½ fl oz)	neg	135	neg
Orange, whole	150 g (5 oz)	10 g	40	2.3 g
Orange juice	100 ml (4 fl oz)	10 g	40	neg
Papaya (flesh only)	80 g (3 oz)	10 g	40	0.4 g
Passionfruit	285 g (10 oz)	10 g	63	2.2 g
Peach, fresh whole	125 g (4½ oz)	10 g	40	1.5 g
Peanut butter, natural	25 g (1 oz)	5 g	160	1.9 g
Pear	130 g (4½ oz)	10 g	40	2.2 g
Pecan nuts, shelled	165 g (5½ oz)	10 g	1120	8.2 g
Pineapple, fresh (flesh only)	90 g (3½ oz)	10 g	40	1.1 g
Pistachio nuts, shelled	65 g (2½ oz)	10 g	407	n/a
Plums, dessert	110 g (4 oz)	10 g	40	2.2 g
Pomegranate	130 g (4½ oz)	10 g	42	2.9 g
Poppy seeds	25 g (1 oz)	5 g	140	n/a
Potato, mashed (no milk, butter)	50 g (2 oz)	10 g	40	0.5 g
Prunes, dried, no stones	25 g (1 oz)	10 g	35	3.4 g
Pumpkin, cooked	100 g (4 oz)	1 g	10	0.6 g
Pumpkin seeds	25 g (1 oz)	5 g	140	1.0 g
Quark, skimmed milk	50 g (2 oz)	3 g	40	neg
Raisins	15 g (½ oz)	10 g	35	1.0 g
Raspberries	175 g (6 oz)	10 g	45	13.3 g
Redcurrants	225 g (8 oz)	10 g	45	16 g

Rice, brown	25 g (1 oz)	20 g	90	0.2 g
Rice flakes, brown	25 g (1 oz)	20 g	90	0.2 g
Ricotta cheese	100 g (4 oz)	2 g	145	0
Rose water	25 ml (1 fl oz)	neg	neg	neg
Rye flour	25 g (1 oz)	19 g	85	n/a
Semolina, wholewheat	25 g (1 oz)	8 g	55	5.0 g
Sesame seeds	25 g (1 oz)	5 g	145	1.3 g
Sharonfruit, flesh only	55 g (2 oz)	10 g	41	0.9 g
Shredded wheat	1 bar	18 g	80	3.3 g
Soya milk	200 ml (7 fl oz)	7 g	210	neg
Starfruit	135 g (4½ oz)	10 g	41	2.3 g
Strawberries, fresh	160 g (5½ oz)	10 g	40	3.5 g
Sugar-free jam (apricot/ plum/raspberry)	30 g (1 oz)	10 g	38	n/a
Sultanas	15 g (½ oz)	10 g	40	1.0 g
Sunflower seeds	25 g (1 oz)	5 g	140	0.9 g
Tahini (sesame seed paste)	25 g (1 oz)	5 g	145	1.3 g
Tayberries	175 g (6 oz)	10 g	44	n/a
Tofu (soya bean curd)	100 g (4 oz)	3 g	55	neg
Walnuts, shelled	25 g (1 oz)	neg	130	1.3 g
Watermelon	190 g (6½ oz)	10 g	38	1.7 g
Wheat germ	25 g (1 oz)	11 g	85	n/a
Yogurt: Greek	250 g (8 oz)	10 g	335	0
live	140 g (4¾ oz)	10 g	77	0
natural, low-fat	150 ml (5 fl oz)	10 g	80	neg

Select Bibliography

Action and Information on Sugars, *Exposing the Sweet Talk: a critique and briefing paper on the Sugar Bureau's teaching pack 'Science and Technology for Seasonal Celebrations'*. 1991

— *The Regulation of Television Advertising: children and sweetened foods*. 1991

Cohen, A. M., 'Change of diet of Yemenite Jews in relation to diabetes and ischaemic heart-disease', *The Lancet*, 23 December 1961

Cooper, Derek, *The Food Programme*, BBC Radio 4, 27 March 1987

Department of Health, *Dietary Sugars and Human Disease*. Report of the Panel on Dietary Sugars. Committee on Medical Aspects of Food Policy. HMSO, 1989

— *The Health of the Nation: a Consultative Document for Health in England*. HMSO, 1991

— *Dietary Reference Values for Food Energy and Nutrients for the United Kingdom*. Report of the Panel on Dietary Reference Values of the Committee on Medical Aspects of Food Policy. HMSO, 1991

Edington, J., *et al.*, 'Effects of dietary cholesterol on plasma cholesterol concentration in subjects following reduced fat, high fibre diet', *British Medical Journal*, 7 February 1987

Greenwood, John, 'Sugar content of liquid prescription medicines', *Pharmaceutical Journal*, 28 October 1989

Health Education Authority, *Enjoy Healthy Eating*. HMSO, 1991

Heaton, K. W. 'Sugars in human disease: a review of the evidence' in *Human Nutrition: a continuing debate*, ed. M. A. Eastwood *et al.* Chapman and Hall, 1992

Lebrecht, Elbie, 'Eating to be wafer thin', *Sunday Times* Magazine July 1990

Lefever, Robert, *How to Combat Anorexia, Bulimia and Compulsive Overeating: the Promis handbook on eating disorders and recovery.* London, 1988

McGee, Harold, *On Food and Cooking: the science and lore of the kitchen.* Unwin Hyman, 1987

Metcalfe, M. A., and Baum, J. D., 'Incidence of insulin dependent diabetes in children aged under 15 years in the British Isles during 1988', *British Medical Journal*, 23 February 1991

Ministry of Agriculture, Fisheries and Farming, *A Comparison of Methods for the Detection of Different Substances in Orange Juice.* HMSO, 1991

Patterson, C. C., *et al.*, 'Epidemiology of Type I (Insulin-Dependent) Diabetes in Scotland 1968–1976: evidence of an increasing incidence', *Diabetologia*, vol. 24, 1983

Paul, A. A., and Southgate, D. A. T., *McCance and Widdowson's The Composition of Foods.* HMSO, 1978

Roberts, H. J., *Aspartame (Nutrasweet): Is it safe?* Philadelphia, The Charles Press, 1990

Rogers, P. J., and Blundell, J. E., 'Separating the actions of sweetness and calories: effects of saccharin and carbohydrates on hunger and food intake in human subjects', *Physiology and Behaviour*, vol. 45

Shaw, Neil, 'Ambassador who sweet-talks for sugar', *The Times*, 25 May 1991

Which?, 'Pesticide residues', October 1990.

World Health Organization, *Diet, Nutrition and the Prevention of Chronic Diseases.* Geneva, 1990

Index

Win a Luxury Ice Cream Maker!

Win your own Prima Ariete 692 Ice Cream Maker to make the delicious ice cream recipes in this book. Retailing at £249.99, this is a top-of-the-range model with a 1.6 litre capacity and a built-in refrigeration unit.

Six runners-up will receive the new deluxe Prima Multi-Purpose Blender System (retailing at £39.95), complete with three interchangeable blades. All prizes for this competition were kindly donated by Prima Appliance Marketing Limited, Prima House, 4–6 Hanworth Road, Low Moor, Bradford BD12 0SG.

Just write out your answers to the following questions on a postcard with your name address and send to:

Promotions Department
Faber and Faber Publishers Ltd
London WCIN 3AU

The closing date is 1 January 1994. The prizewinners will be the first seven postcards with all the answers correct to be picked out of the postbag.

1 White and brown sugar contain the following amount of vitamin C per 100 grams –
   a) 4 mg
   b) 0 mg
   c) 0.8 mg

2 The WHO Report recommends cutting sugar intake from 20 per cent to –
   a) 0–10 per cent
   b) 15 per cent
   c) 12.5 per cent

3 Which of the following sweeteners is highest in fibre?
   a) sugar
   b) dried apricots
   c) bananas

4 Raw cane sugar contains the following amount of white
   sugar –
   a) 3 per cent
   b) 50 per cent
   c) around 98 per cent

5 On every working day in England and Wales, how many
   children under five undergo a general anaesthetic for
   teeth to be removed?
   a) 90
   b) 50
   c) 110

6 What is the percentage of fat in double cream?
   a) 48.2 per cent
   b) 21.2 per cent
   c) 35.1 per cent